CARLETON VARNEY DECORATES WINDOWS
Carleton B. Varney, Jr.

CHL CREATIVE HOME LIBRARY®
In Association with Better Homes and Gardens®
Meredith Corporation

CHL CREATIVE HOME LIBRARY®

© 1975 by Meredith Corporation, Des Moines, Iowa
All rights reserved
Printed in the United States of America

Library of Congress Cataloging in Publication Data

Varney, Carleton.
   Carleton Varney decorates windows.

  1. Interior decoration. 2. Windows. I. Title.
TX315.V37   645'.3   74-14807
ISBN 0-696-14500-6

**CARLETON VARNEY
DECORATES WINDOWS**

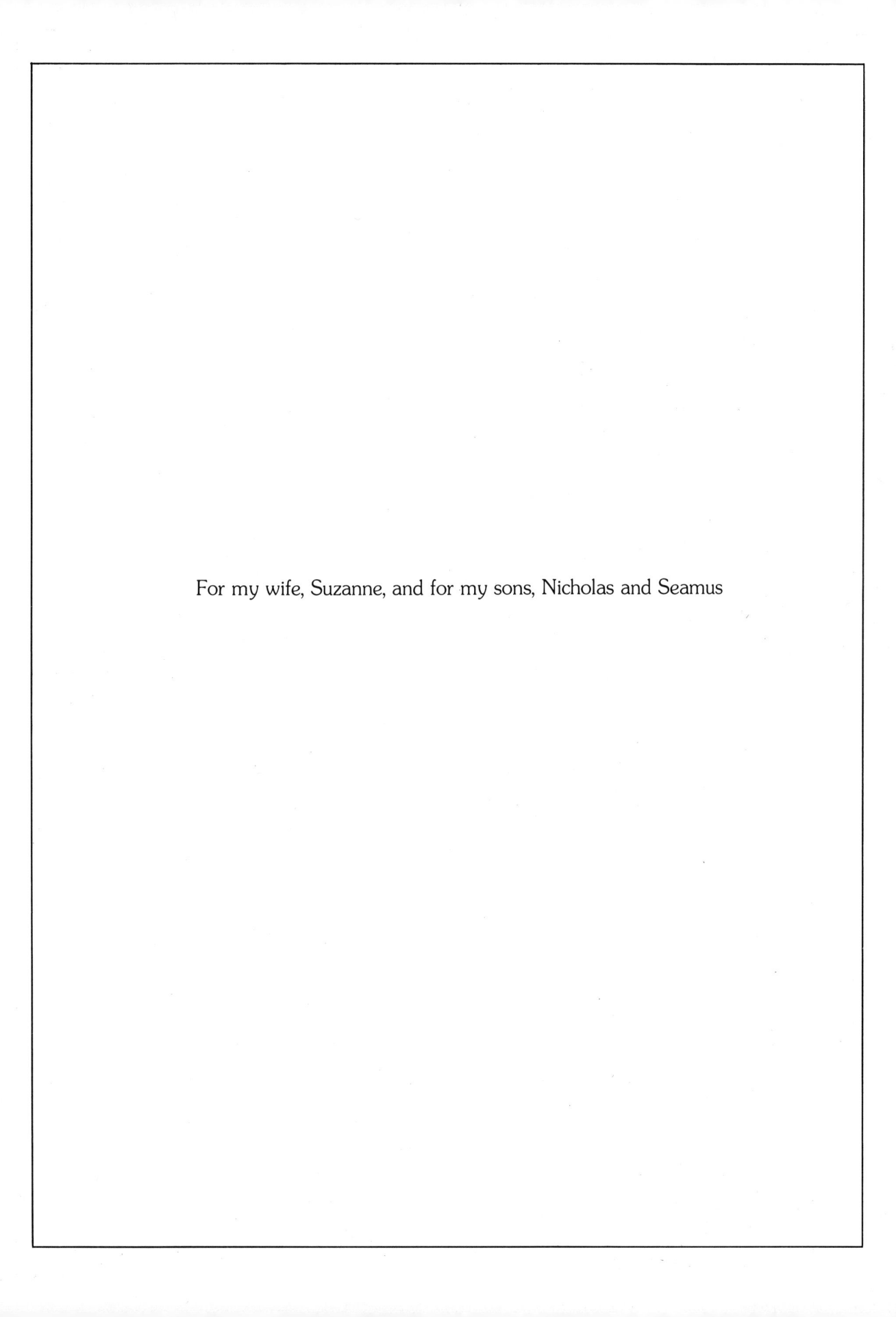

For my wife, Suzanne, and for my sons, Nicholas and Seamus

Contents

Introduction	11
Chapter 1: Living Room and Family Room Window Treatments	19
Chapter 2: Bedroom Window Treatments	43
Chapter 3: Kitchen and Dining Room Window Treatments	63
Chapter 4: Bathroom Window Treatments	83
Chapter 5: Special or Problem Window Treatments	91
Chapter 6: A Picture Dictionary of Period Window Treatments	109
Chapter 7: How to Make Your Own Window Treatments for Every Room in the Home	125
A Glossary of Window Decorating Terms	135
Index	142

About the Author

Listed in *Who's Who in America,* Carleton Varney is an interior decorator, painter, lecturer, and author. He is President of Dorothy Draper and Company, Inc., a well-known interior decorating firm in New York, and author of the nationally syndicated newspaper column, "Your Family Decorator." Other books written by Carleton Varney include *The Family Decorates a Home, You and Your Apartment,* and *Decorating with Color.* Varney's decorating achievements range from country clubs, corporations, banks, and private homes to great hotels, such as the Greenbrier in White Sulphur Springs, West Virginia and the Sheraton-Waikiki, the world's largest convention hotel in Honolulu, Hawaii. Varney has been a recipient of the Design Achievement Award and is a member of the American Institute of Industrial Designers.

Introduction

During my career as a decorator, I have observed that many people would rather jump out a window than decorate one! They get scared by all that hardware: the rods, the poles, the hooks, the rings. Home decorators who might calmly consider the pros and cons of a particular investment, the purchase of a new family car, or the planning of a menu for the boss and his wife retreat in horror at the prospect of choosing window treatments for their own living rooms or bedrooms! Or worse, they often settle for dull, unimaginative, bland window treatments, which look like yesterday's mashed potatoes, because they are under the illusion that the kind of window treatments they would really like would cost an arm and a leg.

Believe me, you don't have to settle for ordinary window displays. Imaginative window treatments—that decorating element that sets the tone of your entire room—are painless to achieve. Even all-thumbs home decorators on slim budgets can do it. Take it from me, whipping up a window treatment of your dreams is *fun!*

In this book, I hope to demonstrate—once and for all—with clear, step-by-step instructions, how window decoration can be an exciting, rewarding project that any home decorator can undertake successfully. In addition to many window ideas, the following pages will present all the information you need to create window treatments that will more than rival those costing hundreds of dollars more. No matter what your budget or style preference may be, there is something for you.

The most important consideration in window decoration—in all home decoration, for that matter—is You, with a capital Y. A window can be anything you want it to be; it all depends on your taste, your personality, your idea of who you are as an individual or as a family, and how you want the world to see you. You will have to decide how you want to see the world, too, of course, for window treatments can bring in a view you want to relish, close out a view you could do without, or provide any combination of choices in between.

Here is a simple example of some of the different moods and effects a window treatment can create on a typical "Plain Jane American" sash window.

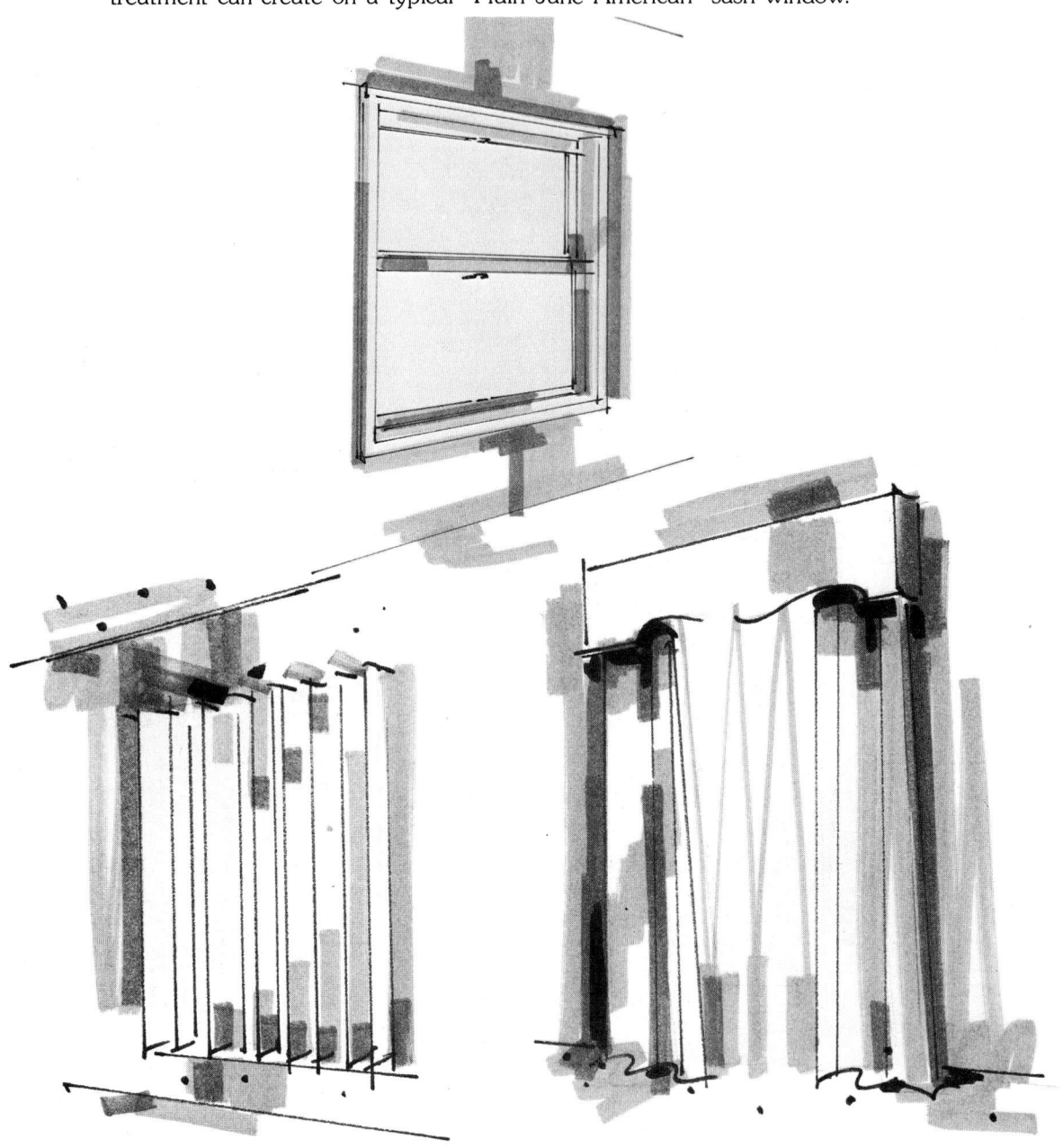

Here's the same window with vertical blinds, as decorated by a modernist with a yen for the tailored look. *(Left)*

And here it is done up in elegant fashion to admit an elegant view, using a shaped valance, stationary tieback draperies, and sheer undercurtains. *(Right)*

The same window in a bedroom could be made to look super masculine. *(Left)* Or super feminine. *(Right)*

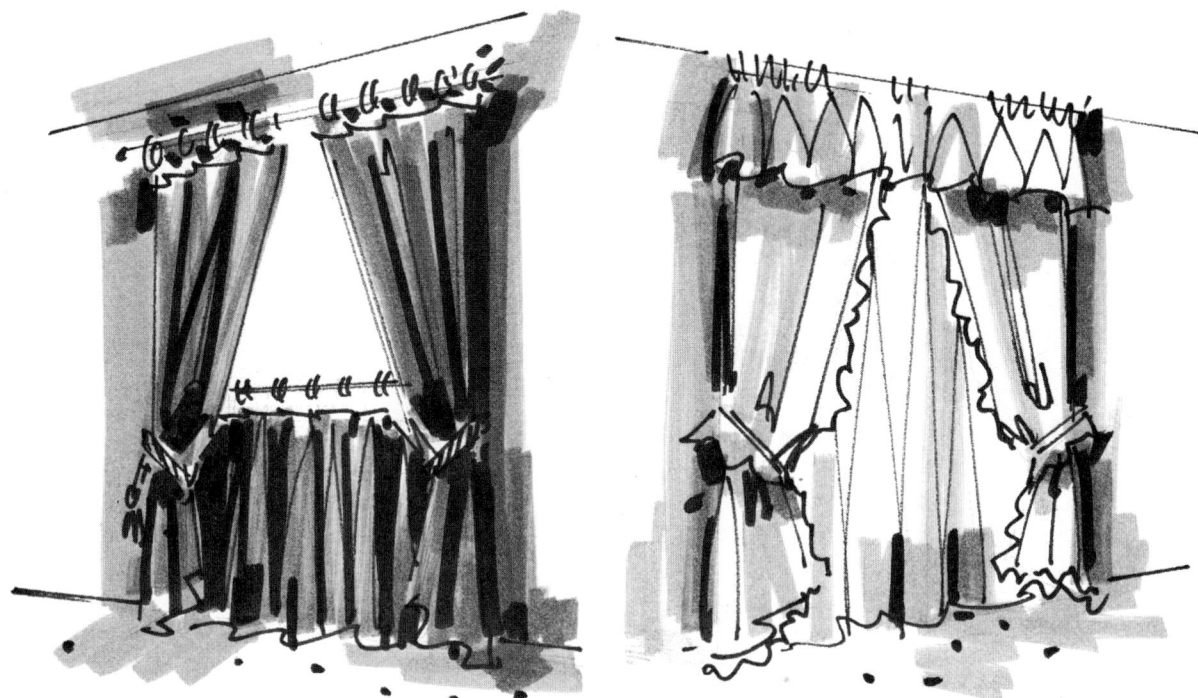

So whether you have a view that rivals Versailles's, a pleasant country landscape, a row of city trees and houses, or a stark brick wall outside your window, the draperies, shades, screens, or shutters you choose to bring that view inside (or keep it out) will go a long way toward setting the tone of your living space. There is, in my mind, no other single focal point that will coordinate a room as easily, or as inexpensively, as the window treatment.

You and Your Family

The Bachelor Years . . .

Let's begin by finding out about your taste and style. Are you a swinging single living in temporary quarters? In my bachelor days, I wanted lots of flair and style, but I didn't want to spend a king's ransom on temporary quarters. For all you bachelors and bachelor girls who feel as I did, there's good news for your windows in this book. I will show you how dime-store fabrics; snappy, inexpensive tailored shades; simple roller shades; or slinky, exotic bead treatments can give the windows of your singles' pad a fresh, original, and custom-made look—for pennies!

For Budget-Conscious Newlyweds

Or, perhaps you are newlyweds, just starting out in your first house or apartment. I know many young couples with limited budgets who, nevertheless, have unlimited hopes of creating a spectacular effect in their home. And why not? Of course, you'll begin with your windows. Believe me, every window in your nest can be decorated beautifully on your newlywed budget with simple basic treatments and accessories, ranging from rickrack to hardware store chains. Once I've shown you how to make a basic drape and valance, you can improvise to your heart's content! I'll also show you how durable shades can be appliquéd, stenciled, or painted to create custom looks that are yours alone. From now on, every time you pass an expensive home-furnishing display that offers less-imaginative treatments at twice the cost, your secret smile will stretch from ear to ear.

The Family Grows . . .

Perhaps you've passed those newlywed years, started a family, and moved to larger quarters. Your new home probably has lots more windows—windows that let the sun into the nursery, windows that hold your son's rock and mineral collection, windows that house air conditioners for summer comfort. I will show you how to create window treatments to conceal those unsightly air-conditioning eyesores. I will show you how to create window treatments that will maximize the sunshine coming into a room. I will show you how to create window treatments that will close out the world when you want privacy.

As Family Needs Change

Or, perhaps your children have passed through the chocolate-fingered stage and have begun the rock-and-roll years. Lucky you! You've outgrown the need for "childproof" home decorations and can start thinking about giving your home a face-lift. What better place to start than with the windows? I will show you how you can "teen up" a window treatment as easily as your rock-and-rollers stack records on their stereo sets.

And I'll show you how to make simple window valances and frames that can transform a nursery playroom into a "with-it" hangout. The kids will be able to entertain their friends out of earshot.

For You and Him Alone

Or, perhaps you are in the enviable position of having children who are grown up and out on their own. Bills for braces, summer camp, and college are a thing of the past. Perhaps your home, if you've bought one, is mortgage-free—which means that you're free, too! It's time for travel, for resuming old careers, or for picking up new interests. It's also time for a new look at your home. Why not begin by looking at the windows?

Face-Lifting the Family Home . . .

Perhaps you and your husband are sentimentalists at heart. You have decided to stay put, just the two of you, in your family home. The space that began as a family room—complete with playpen, toy chest, pegboard walls, and durable, no-nonsense window treatments—can now be converted into a dormitory for all those visiting grandchildren. With the same furniture, carpeting, and accessories, you can create a room that your grandchildren will clamor to visit. Use your imagination at the windows. Try stuffed toys as drapery tiebacks or install louver shutters, paint them in horizontal rainbow stripes, and continue the design right onto the walls and around the room. A ruler and a few small cans of paint in rainbow hues is all you'll need.

The Second Honeymoon Nest

Perhaps you and your husband have decided to move to a small, modern efficiency apartment in some warm, sunny clime. It will be the first time in a long time that you've had to deal with all that new, bare space. Now is the time of your life when you can indulge yourself in those window fabrics, treatments, and accessories that budget and circumstances prevented before.

Begin with the windows and build around them, using such materials as antique hardware, velvets and brocades, sculpted valances, quilted frames, and Japanese screens. The window decor becomes the focal point around which you can gather together the possessions of a lifetime and create a living space that sums up the real You.

With the treatments you learn to create from this book, you will be able to decorate a room in which those precious family heirlooms will be right at home with your Swedish modern furniture. Now is the time to take those prized antique heirlooms down from the attic, where you stored them out of harm's way, and create a window treatment that makes those antiques "come alive."

Picture this: A bay window lightly screened with translucent silk that is over-draped with the smoothest, most luxurious velvet and tied back with eighteenth-century ornaments. Now add a perfect copy of the kind of valance grandma had to your picture. This can be done easily in the most modern apartment or, as you will see, in any type of home you and your husband choose.

His Own Private Place . . .

Moving to other areas of your second-honeymoon nest, isn't it about time that Dad had a quiet study to call his own? A place where he can plan your world travels or read all those books he never had time for before? Why not take one of the spare bedrooms and turn it into a private place for Dad? Do you have an empty room to go to work on? How about setting that almost-antique desk you picked up at an auction at an angle in front of the window? Install rich, neutral gray linen draperies, lined in sunshine yellow and valanced with an understated panel to match a gray and yellow scheme.

For a man with an interest in things Oriental, why not screen his study window with Oriental-style black lacquer panels inset with paper or Chinese-design fabric in striking Chinese red, bronze, black, orange, and Pacific blue? When closed, those screens will make his den mighty cozy and they'll be downright handsome when opened to frame the den window, too. Your family's interests can inspire many ideas, all of which can be translated into your own special window treatments.

For You and You Alone

And what about a private place all *your* own, Mom? Most women I know have that secret craving. And now that women are expressing themselves in so many new and exciting ways, let me tell you that you're entitled to your desires. Whether you want to paint, write, weave, sew—whatever your secret ambition may be—now is the time to begin.

That spare room you've been using for storing odds and ends can be fixed up to lift your spirits high, high, high! And you will be rejuvenated, too, once you've carted your useless odds and ends to Good Will and started—at the window—to create a place of your own. Throw away those curtains you chose for the kids; express your own new personality by creating a window treatment that has to please no one but you. Treat those windows with stained-glass panels. Buy them in an antique shop and hang them from the ceiling with strong cord, or design those stained-glass beauties yourself, using colored acetate sheets, available in any art supply store. Then sit back and watch the sunshine passing through your windows create soft rainbows of color on your walls and ceilings.

The Sky's the Limit . . .

Creating a space for yourself will probably inspire you to think of imaginative window treatments for the rest of your house. This can be done with a minimum investment. Valance your living room windows in sheet mirror and hang straight panels of boldly patterned Scandinavian fabric in place of those old faded draperies you've had for years. Install floor-to-ceiling screens in front of the windows. They can be louvered, painted, fabric-backed, mixed, matched, and coordinated to vary the entire living room without your having to buy so much as a new slipcover.

Now Let's Begin . . .

Turn the page and start exploring the many window treatments contained in the pages that follow:

In Chapter 1, you will find living room and family room treatments for every taste, budget, window style, and life-style.

Chapter 2 is given over to my favorite area of window decorations—the bedroom. I love those soft or sleek bedroom window treatments, whether they're for kids or grownups.

If special kitchen and dining room window treatments are what you're looking for, look no farther than Chapter 3. The windows of the kitchen—that cozy family gathering place in many homes—have lots of potential. And well-created dining room window treatments can enhance a meal from soup to dessert!

Or, maybe a very special look for your bathroom windows is what you seek. You'll find lots of suggestions in Chapter 4.

Is your home a crazy mélange of problem windows that jut, curve, and slant? Perhaps there's just one strangely shaped or oddly placed round, triangular, or curved window that's your nemesis. Chapter 5 was written especially for you!

If you're a history buff, Chapter 6—a picture dictionary of period window treatments—will keep your inspiration level high.

But don't close the book yet. Turn to Chapter 7 for instructions on how to create many of those super window effects you desire. Every window treatment in this book is simple to make. Some are special on my list of preferences, however, so I've decided to show you how to make them, step-by-step, in this section.

And if strange terms and words trip you up along the way, the glossary in the very back of the book is the place to look them all up.

I've enjoyed writing this book of window treatments. I hope you enjoy reading it. I think it's unique, and I know it's useful! But what's more important, I hope that you'll enjoy dressing up your windows, using my book as an inspiration, a guide, and a reference.

Happy window decorating!

Chapter 1

Living Room and Family Room Window Treatments

Of all the windows in your home, living room or family room windows are usually the first ones that visitors see—and they should say lots about You! They represent, therefore, the greatest decorating challenge and the widest range of possible treatments. In the living room and family room, you're not necessarily limited by the same need for privacy as you are in the bedroom or bathroom. And you're not as limited by the need for using washable materials as you are in the kitchen or nursery.

Family room windows may call for informal treatment with durable fabric, but a living room window's style is limited only by your imagination and by your budget. As you'll see when you read on, however, a "limited budget" does not, by any means, dictate dull, unattractive window treatments.

The first thing to consider about living and family room window treatments is your personal style of decorating. Is it rustic with a country flavor? Then why not do your living or family room windows with full-length draperies of coarsely woven cotton? Those rough-textured fabrics look great against stucco walls or weathered barn siding.

Make a trellis valance for a light and airy living room window. With semigloss enamel, paint the frame and the fretwork white. The paint should be of an oil base. Behind the fretwork valance frame, hang white undercurtains and an overdrapery of a floral print—perhaps a print design, featuring green leaves and yellow, orange, and lavender flowers against a white background. Use the same drapery print (quilted) as the fabric on white wicker lounge chairs. (*Left*)

Dull, ordinary family room windows might call for a frame with a beamed effect, created with ordinary plywood that has been stained, by you, to give the whole room flavor and atmosphere. Back your frame with pleated white duck, and you'll think that you're rusticating in a chic Vermont barn.

Since the living room and family room are the rooms where your family and guests gather, they should, naturally, reflect your taste. But style is not enough. There's a budget to consider as well. I maintain that you can have elegant living and family room treatments even on a slim budget—if you know how to do it. I'll show you how.

One thing I dislike, particularly for living rooms, is a skimpy window treatment. It's as bad as no window treatment at all—and sometimes, it's much worse! The skimpy window treatment comes about when the decorator—probably you—makes the mistake of selecting a drapery fabric she can't really afford. To make ends meet, she skimps on yardage. It's a little bit like buying expensive fabric to make a dress and then discovering you don't have enough to make the second sleeve!

I always insist that if a client can't afford enough of an expensive drapery fabric, she's better off choosing less-costly yardage. Then she can go wild, using yards and yards of it. The effect is always far more luxurious in the end. I've seen opulent-looking window treatments for living rooms that were done in inexpensive Indian prints. In one such room, the print fabric was shirred on the walls and used for tieback draperies and valances, too. The fabric was inexpensive, but the look was fit for a raja! I've also seen Early American window treatments done for a family room, with yards and yards of dime-store gingham. And it was as pretty as a picture, despite the humble price tag.

If your taste runs to the elegant period but your budget isn't quite as lavish as your decorating fantasies, why not use the elegant fabric of your choice on laminated window shades? Add a luxurious scalloped border. Don't forget to include gleaming filigree pulls for opening and closing those laminated shades.

I've indicated here some of the ways in which you can achieve living and family room window treatments that fall into your style and budget. Don't forget, however, that a window treatment must also suit the style of your windows. There are lucky people who have windows that let in a glorious view—windows that probably should have no window treatment at all. There are other fortunate people whose old homes have stained-glass windows of great distinction. No window treatments are necessary for them, either!

Then there are less-fortunate folk whose outside "view" consists of an air shaft or a flashing neon sign. They definitely need window treatments of the most permanent type. Shutters, screens, or dead-hung drapery panels running clear across the windows would be my choice.

Finally, when planning your living room window treatments, you should consider the way *you* live. If you have a few rough-and-tumble youngsters around, you'll want to think twice about succumbing to the temptation of those luscious pastel brocade draperies. A set of washable draperies would be more up your alley while the children are young.

If you have a cat—or two, or three—and he assumes that your draperies were put up for his own personal scratching pleasure, you should consider something less destructible and more durable, such as shutters, screens, or venetian blinds.

Remember, a drapery treatment is beautiful only when it is useful, too. You will soon grow to view your beautiful new draperies with less than love if you discover that they are incompatible with the way you live.

So, before you dress up your living room and family room windows and before you turn the page to read about the treatments I've designed for those rooms, consider four basic facts of life: your taste and preferences, your budget, your windows and the view beyond, and your life-style.

Take each factor into consideration before you invest in draperies, shades, screens, or whatever. A little planning and forethought will make the final product—your beautiful living room and family room windows—a lot more enjoyable, useful, and durable.

Giving a barn look to your family room is possible, even in a city apartment. Cover the concrete soffit and side wall soffits with a wood-grain vinyl, or even a wood-grain wallpaper. You can give the soffit a *faux bois* look with paint if you have a lot of patience. *Faux bois*, incidentally, means "fake wood." By installing uprights (wood members), you can create a barn roof design. Wood members should either be painted in the *faux bois* manner or covered with wood-grain vinyl or paper. Behind the barn-wood-motif focal point hangs box-pleated drapery of white duck.

Much can be done to make the window wall the focal point of a family room by using standard 1 × 12 pine planks. Here, bookcases have been created for the look of a modern library. By using three bookcase sections, two windows have been created. The units are decorated with accessories and connected by 1 × 12 pine plank valances. All woodwork is stained walnut, and curtains are of a white, washable, open-weave casement. I feel that casement drapery fabric is ideal for creating the new look of lace.

Oh, that classic look! Did you know that you can buy Doric, Ionic, and Corinthian columns from lumber dealers? Custom heights can be specially ordered. Think of what four columns with a plywood soffit, onto which stock half-round molding has been applied, can do for your wall. Your center panel might very well be sheet-mirrored. Between the columns and behind the white-painted plywood soffit hang sheer white undercurtains. If colored sheers are your bent, choose a color that matches the wall paint shade and a pair of tied-back overdraperies.

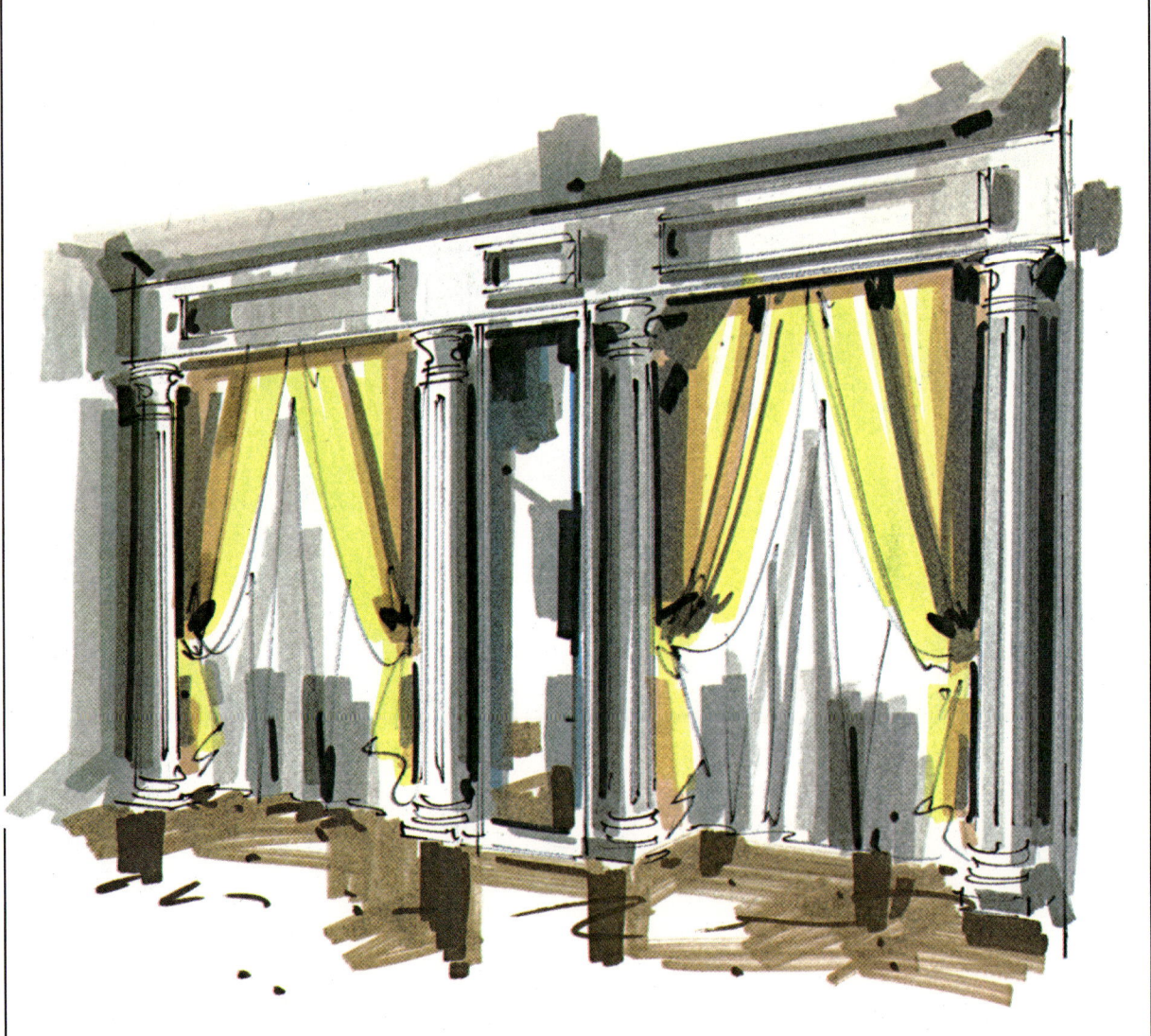

If you have a bay window in your living room, use the floor space area to place a furniture grouping—perhaps a skirted table and a pair of upholstered, wood-frame chairs. I have seen bay windows treated with card table groupings, with plant and sculpture arrangements, and with a kidney-shaped desk and a small bench. This bay window valance and drapery is installed across the front of the bay, not along the contour. The contour shown here has been graced with washable white sheers.

Why not appliqué a flowery design onto your living room or family room window shade? Motifs cut from fabrics or wallpapers can be pasted on a cloth shade very easily. Decals and flexible stick-ons can make exciting appliqués, too!

For the family room, the built-in units above, below, and at the sides of the air conditioner create a finished look. I like the look best when the air-conditioning (or heating) unit is the same color and finish as the shelving and lower cabinets. The built-in units in this illustration are white plastic laminate. Curtains, made of unlined, royal blue glosheen, are hung on a brass pole with brass rings in the newly created window.

Decorate the entire window wall of your living room with white vertical blinds. The blinds can be turned left or right to regulate light and view. In this room, vertical blinds offer height to the low, 8½-foot ceiling. Note also how well they blend into a room furnished with a mixture of traditional and modern.

Roman shades can make the windows in your family room take on lots of new pizazz. Here, Roman shades are made of a laminated fabric to match the wallpaper. The sofa, placed in front of the window, is also covered in fabric to match the shades. Many people use Roman shades to achieve the country look. Easily installed, they are operated with a cord, rings, and a pulley. When they are raised, deep pleats are created.

They're not building arch windows like they used to—except, maybe in villas on the Italian Mediterranean. What a pity! I've always loved the height and grace of arch windows. There are still a few lucky people, such as dwellers of America's Georgian houses, who are fortunate enough to have this graceful window treatment in their apartments or homes.

To those fortunate few, my advice is to cover all the wall surfaces, at the sides and at the top of the arched window, with a gracious fabric. For the drapery, use a matching fabric.

The arched window in the illustration is decorated with a red, blue, green, and melon print on a dark beige background. The draperies are pinch-pleated and are installed from ceiling to floor on pull-cord traverse rods. The walls are covered with fabric to match the drapery. *(Left)*

Tortoise-finished matchstick blinds can be utilized for a formal look in the living room and for the woodsy den–library look in the family room. *(Right)*

No matter what the style of your room—modern or traditional—there are a number of painting techniques that will work effectively on shades. This freehand black-on-white geometric pattern certainly gives this living room a contemporary feeling.

This window design graces the assembly room at Gadsky's Tavern, Virginia, built in 1793. A reproduction is on view at the Metropolitan Museum of Art in New York City. Note how handsome the wood blinds look under the gold and white crown detail. *(Left)*

Here, we have the handsome, tailored look of Roman shades. A large window is made to seem smaller by adding three 1 × 2 wood uprights and staining them fruitwood. Roman shades, installed within the frames, are a tangerine, green, and beige linen stripe. When pulled to the top, the shades will stack under a bought Roman shade valance, some 8 inches deep. *(Right)*

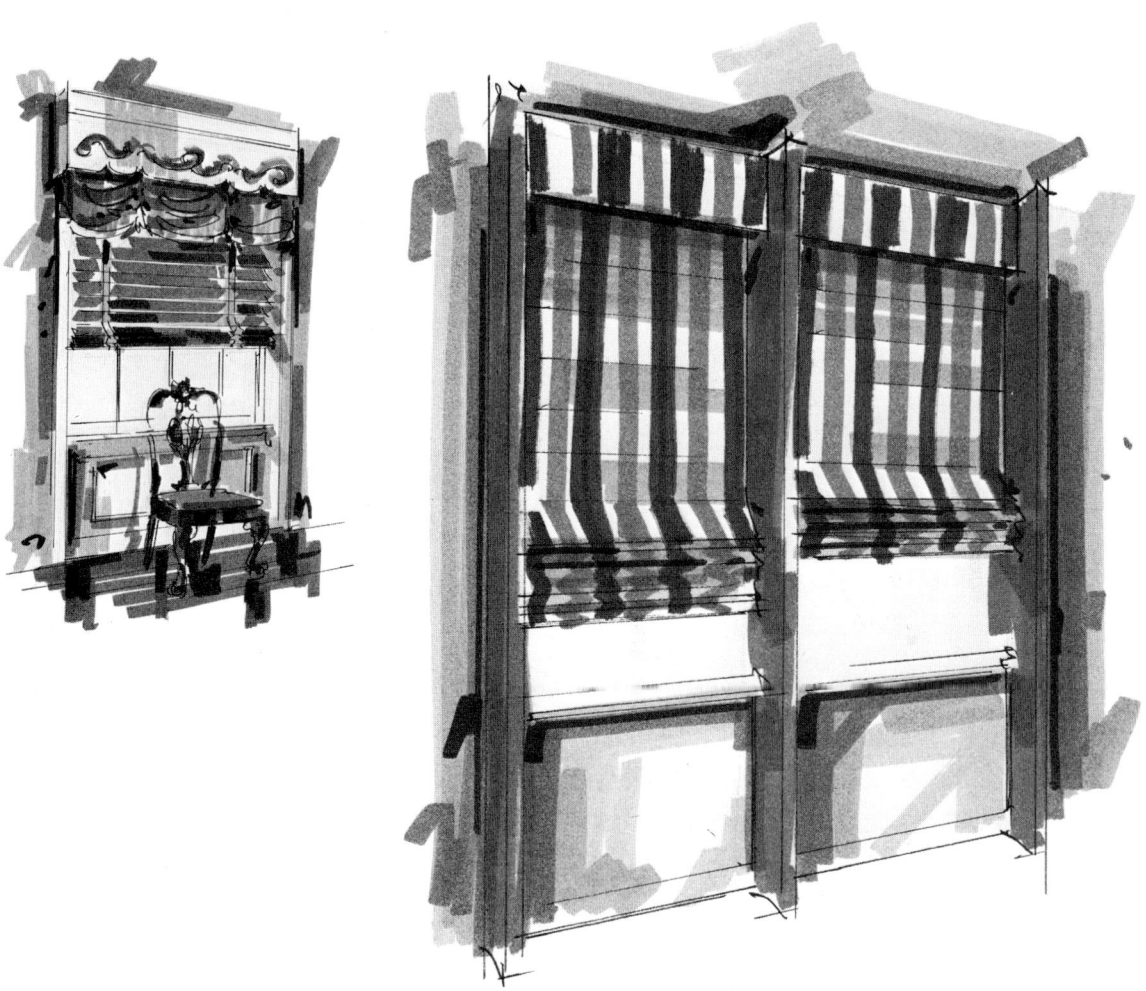

For the informal family room look, try using matchstick tortoise roll-up blinds. This sheet-glass picture window in a country house displays the effectiveness of such a treatment. *(Left)*

A budget window treatment features colored glass beads that glisten in the sunlight. I like glass-beaded curtains best when they are hung in front of a white or translucent window shade. *(Right)*

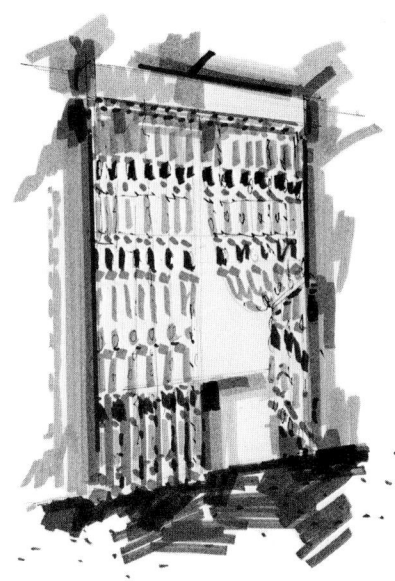

For the elegant look, try a white silk fabric swag, hung over a bronze pole with pineapple finial ends. The underdraperies shown here are made of silk. This drapery design can be used throughout the home, incidentally, and looks best with French or formal English furnishings. *(Left)*

For the city family room, where the master of the house displays his gun collection, what about a built-in wall cabinet and display rack around that small window? A formal drapery treatment would not work on such a small window, but a drop-down shade of tortoise matchstick is ideal. *(Right)*

A glass and chrome desk fits in well with this modern family room, whose window treatment features white (or silver) roller shades. For the sides of the window, consider the reflective treatment of double-hinged mirrored screens. The window will look wide...wide...wide as its reflection repeats itself countless times through the mirrored screens. *(Left)*

Looking for a way to treat that window doorway that separates the family room and the patio? Why not apply a design of half-round, 1½-inch-wide bamboo molding around the door frame for a dramatic and slightly sophisticated Oriental touch? Paint the moldings white. The wall surfaces between the moldings can go rich chocolate brown; for the glass portion of the doors, try tortoise-finished matchstick roller blinds. *(Right)*

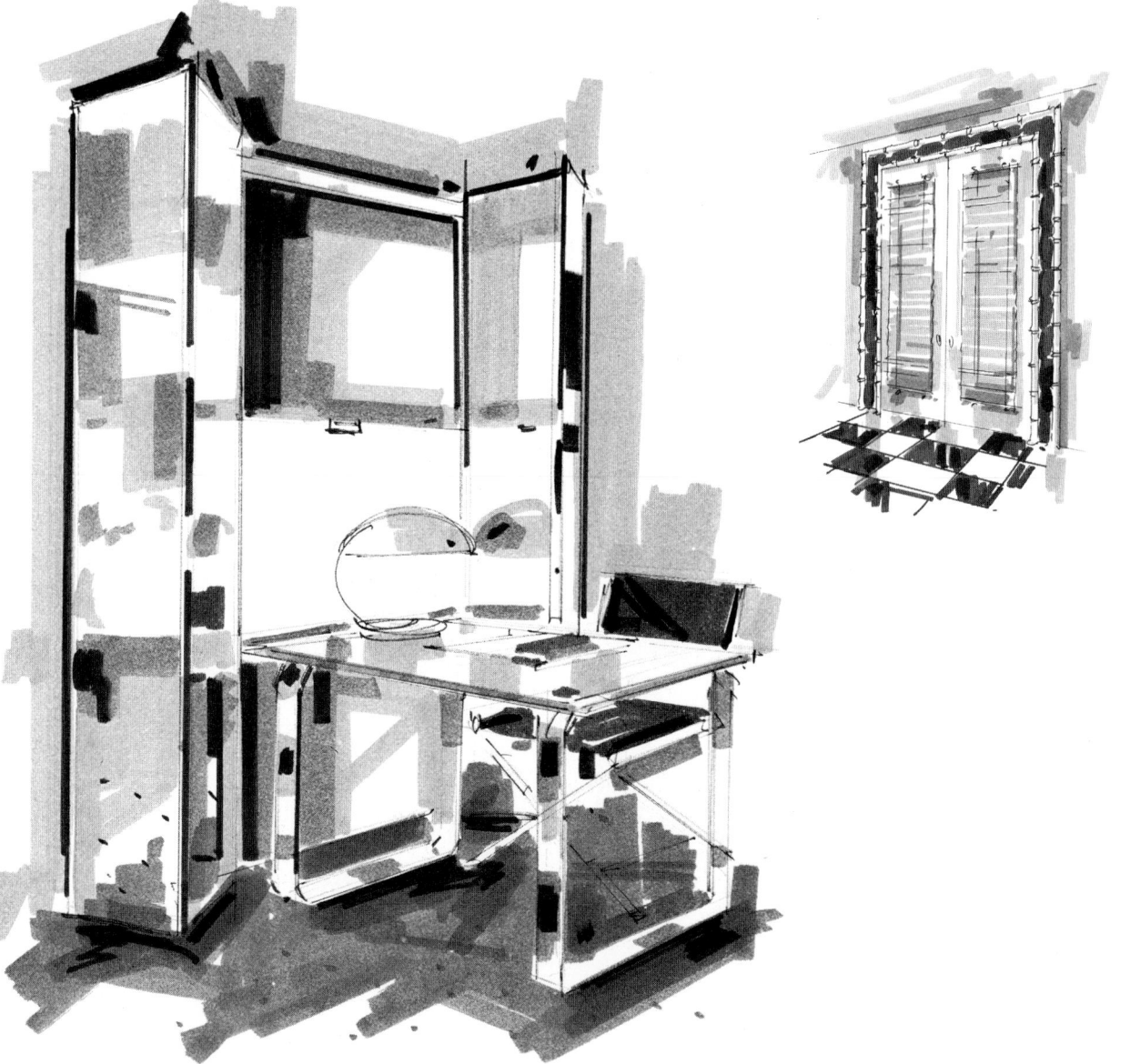

For that touch of formality and a bit of color, you might try trimming a white swag valance with some red velvet ribbon. Here, the window valance and drapery are hung on a finialed pole over sheer white undercurtains. *(Left)*

Do you want a garden look for a small family room window? Make two swing-out frames of stock wood; fill in the frames with lattice, installed on the diagonal. Then hang a roller shade behind your newly created arbor. *(Right)*

If you are a Chippendale enthusiast who wants to place a desk in front of the living or family room window, go mahogany! Maybe you can find a desk with a black leather top. And for that window, what about creating a frame, covered in red, white, and blue horizontal stripes? The lower section of the window can be outfitted with striped cafe curtains, hung on brass poles. At the upper window section, install a red window shade with a shaped bottom.

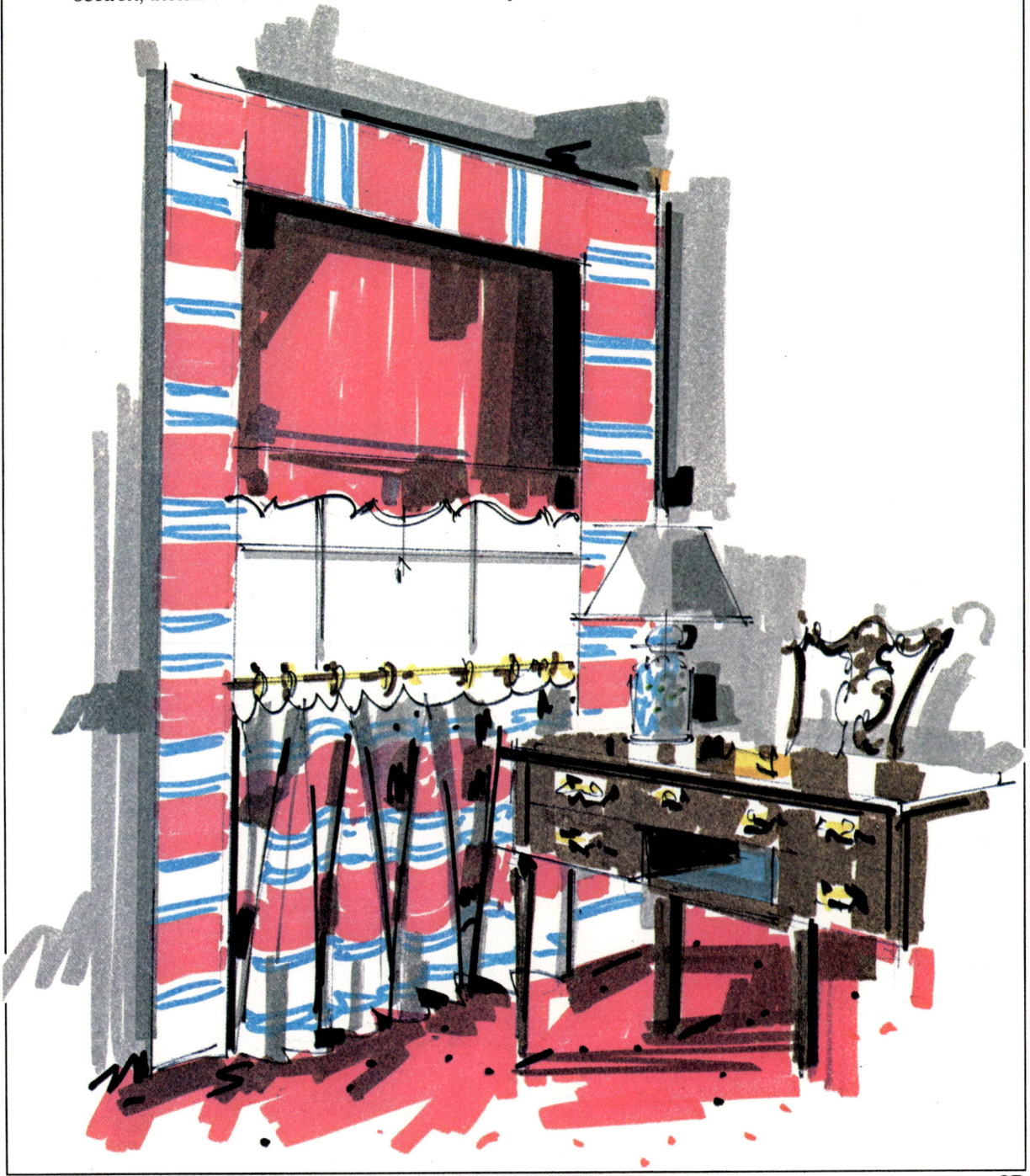

Here's a traditional corner of a family room with a kneehole desk, a comfortable Lawson lounge chair, and a wall of books. For the window treatment, I suggest a walnut valance and draw draperies to the floor. The drapery shown here matches the upholstery on the Lawson club chairs.

A curtain pole can be informally threaded through a flouncy, shirred valance. Here, a green, yellow, and orange geometric print on a white background is hung on a white pole with large, brass ball-end finials. Rings on the white pole are also brass. The stationary drapery panels match the flouncy valance; the undercurtains are made of my favorite white, washable, sheer fabric. *Left)*

For that formal look, try poles! Here, the tied-back gold draperies are hung under a gold, Austrian-styled swag valance, which is hung from brass poles with round, brass finial ends. This window design can be used very dramatically in a variety of traditional room-decorating schemes. *(Right)*

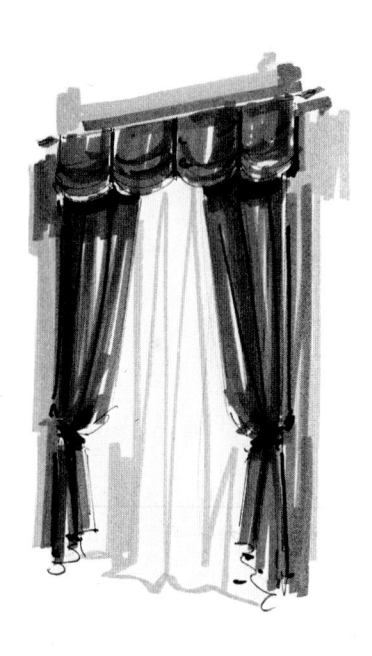

Why cover those small windows in a log cabin country house? The walnut wood mullions are a charming decorative detail. They look so natural and warm with a wood beamed ceiling. Think how awkward and out of character the windows would be if they were valanced and hung with heavy, unneeded draperies! *(Below)*

For the last window in this living room–family room section, here's one of the most elegant no-treatment windows ever designed! Sunburst arch, delicate mullions, Corinthian columns, and a terrific pastoral view outside all combine to say, "No, no treatment please!" How could anyone enhance this beauty? *(Right)*

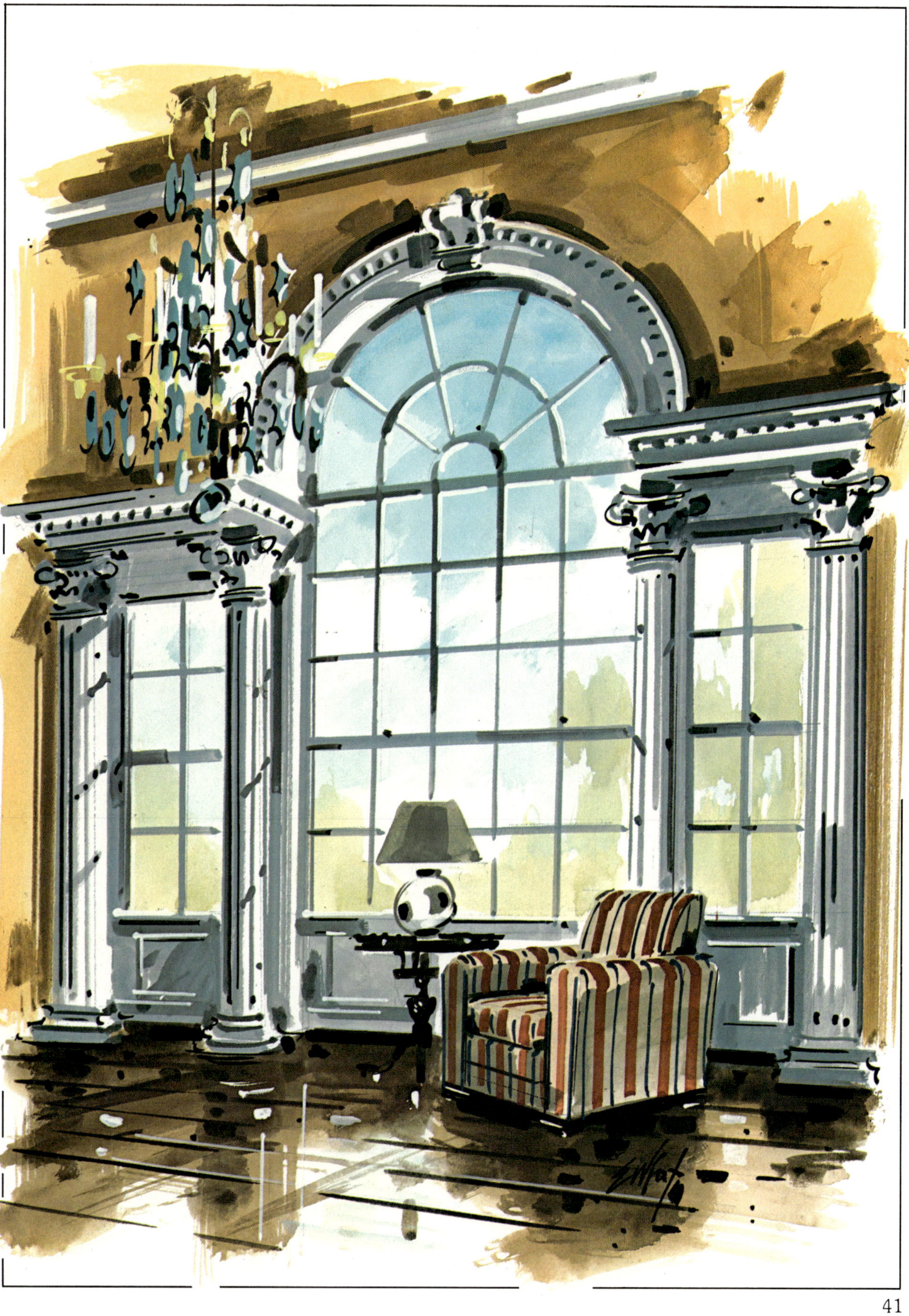

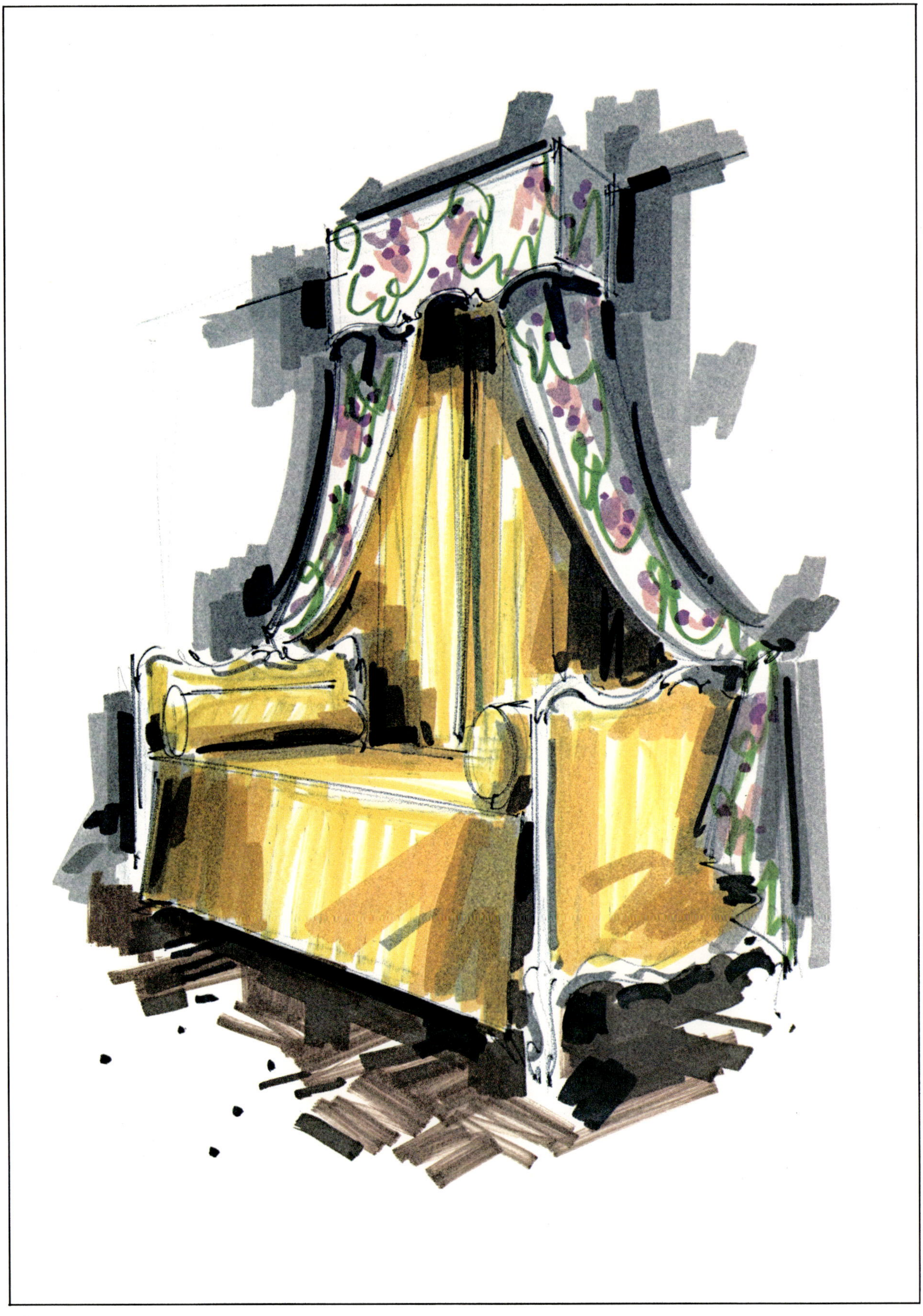

Chapter 2

Bedroom Window Treatments

There's no doubt about it! When it comes to decorating, the bedroom window is my favorite. Whether it be wild and way out or soft and traditional, no other room in the home offers as many opportunities for you to indulge your most personal decorating taste.

Where else but in your bedroom would you be more likely to laze away a Sunday morning with the sun streaming through sheer, softly shirred curtains? Wouldn't you like to spend that lazy Sunday morning tucked under the folds of a canopy that decorates both your window and your bed? And what better place to retire in the evening and put the finishing touches on your latest needlepoint creation? A full window treatment of traverse draperies could make that bedroom a cozy place in which to spend those evening hours.

Your bedroom may have to perform many functions—second family room, study, sleeping quarters, sewing room. With the right window treatment, however, it's easy to integrate all those functions into a harmonious whole. Your bedroom window treatment can be simple or elaborate, casual or formal. It can form a backdrop for your bed or become the backdrop for a quiet conversation area.

Your bedroom window treatment can also frame a desk arrangement. What better place is there for paying bills or writing letters than a bedroom desk, positioned so that you will be able to glance up from time to time to enjoy a pretty view through parted louvers?

For the Marie Antoinette at heart, here's a crowning way to treat the bedroom window. Behind an elegant, white, wooden-framed daybed is a soft rose and green print crown valance, extending the full width of the window. Dead-hung panels of the same fabric cascade around the bed. The crown is lined in yellow, and windows are curtained to the floor in yellow silk. It's an elegant way to hide a window and create a background at the same time. *(Left)*

If you must cope with city noises or if you have a tendency to be a light sleeper, you might like the practicality of having blackout shades in your bedroom. They'll resist even a tropical sun. But practical doesn't mean unattractive—far from it. Room-darkening shades, especially painted ones, can be mighty attractive.

If your bedroom is blessed with a pretty view by day and privacy by night, you can frame out your bedroom window with a soft, floral valance and dead-hung draperies. If you love a sunny bedroom but have nosy neighbors on all sides, double-hung louvers may be for you. The louvers block out the view while letting in the sun. Or, you can install louvers on only the lower half of your bedroom windows and let the sun pour in through the unshuttered top part.

Your teen-aged daughter might relish the royal luxury of a flower-sprigged canopy bed in front of her window. You can create the graceful canopy with fabric alone or, if her bed fits into an alcove, drape three sides of the alcove with a pretty flowered fabric to match her bedspread.

Now that he's outgrown the sailing ship curtains he started out with, your son would probably love a new, masculine window treatment for his bedroom. How about sleek, tailored vertical blinds or a bold, striped Roman shade?

Bedrooms are fun rooms to decorate, and bedroom windows are the number-one stop on your creative decorating express. Make your bedroom whatever you want to make it, but set the tone at your windows!

If you go modern and use this royal blue window shade in your bedroom, why not paint the wall area below the window blue? Continue your blue across the floor with a strip of matching floor carpeting, and paint a window-width stripe above the shade and across the ceiling.

Bedroom decorating can be fun, but when your room has an awkward window situation and the bed must be placed on the window wall, you've got a problem. Here are some window decorating suggestions: When you have to place the bed on the outside wall, try a canopy and undercurtain effect. I'd recommend that the canopy window valance be of a short depth—10 inches at the most. Pick a handsome print for the facing side of the canopy window valance and drapery; line the canopy in the same color that you select for the draw window draperies. The drapery should be lined with milium for blackout control; it can be opened during the day, of course, when sunlight and brightness are desired.

I have always believed the stripe to be the common denominator in decorating, as this pull-down roller shade of laminated fabric proves. It goes with everything. Here, the striped fabric on the laminated shade is modern in feeling and lends height to the bedroom window, too!

For those many modernists who love Roman window shades, keep this treatment in mind for the bedroom picture window. Create a bed alcove with 1 × 12 pieces of stock lumber and install a bright red, green, and white fabric shade within the newly created frame. The headboard set within the frame can be walnut. Give the double bed some punch by adding a bright red spread with green piping.

For the modernist with a double bed located in front of a picture window, why not frame the window with 2 × 4 pieces of ordinary stock lumber? Paint or stain the wood uprights walnut, mahogany, or chocolate brown. Behind the uprights and within the panels install shirred fabric, perhaps, in bright blue, on rods. Fabric on rods can be opened when daylight is desired. The panels can be installed in one piece or they can be hinged so that each panel will open individually.

For the garden-in-the-bedroom look, why not install a white shelf above the air-conditioning unit at window-sill height? The depth of the shelf can be about 14 inches. As a facing on the unit, consider open lattice, painted white, or, perhaps, plywood filigree. All these treatments are open enough to permit air conditioning and heat to operate effectively. The curtains at the windows should be hung to shelf height.

Here's an arched, pelmet design for a master bedroom. The wood pelmet frame is covered with a lavender and pink tulip wallpaper—the same paper used on the walls. Under the pelmet and within its frame, white, Swiss organdy curtains have been installed. The coloring in the wallpaper works effectively with the room's carpeting. I would suggest a master bedspread of lavender and a bedskirt of grass green to go with this window and wall scheme. *(Left)*

Venetian blinds can give a modern touch to a bedroom, too. I like the new, narrow-slatted blinds. Here, in a modern bedroom, a short window has been boxed out with a mirror-covered frame. The bought venetian blinds are white. *(Right)*

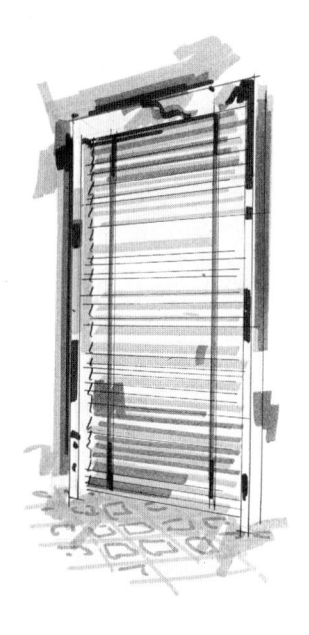

Go casual and install five pine board 1 × 2 members at your bedroom window wall. Secure the members with right-angle braces at the ceiling; use brass rods for bottom curtains. The window shades shown are made of fabric to coordinate with lower cafe curtains. With brass curtain poles, I'd recommend using brass rings. (Be certain to use those brass rings as pulls on the upper shades.)

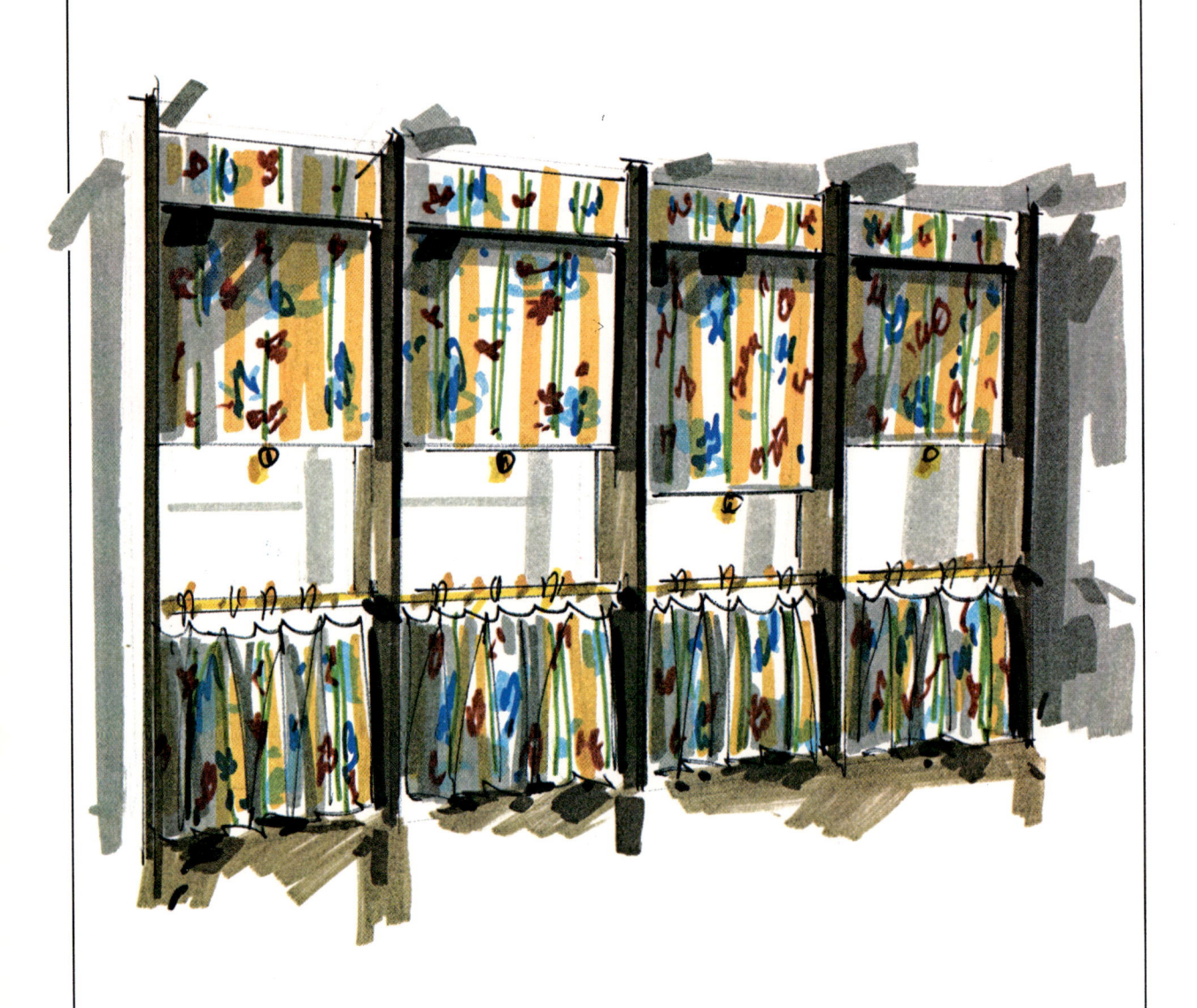

Have you ever considered placing a private wall of folding screens in front of your bedroom windows? The screen can be louvers—painted white, red, or shocking pink—or frames with panels (upper and lower) that are outfitted with stretched fabric. Folding screen walls don't have to be confined to the bedroom. In my own dining room, I have a wall of white lacquered screens with panel openings that are filled with a pink, red, and green flowered pattern on a royal blue background.

Most windows are of the double-hung sash variety, with or without mullions. Modern houses of the 1970s variety seem to be using windows without mullions. However, for a more homey effect, I like windows with mullions best. One of my favorite window treatments, even though many say it's passé, is the criss-cross, organdy-curtained window. I've used criss-cross organdy curtains in every room of the house. I like them best when borders are fluted and ruffled. The ruffled look can be carried right onto the bed canopy and dust ruffle.

Bows are big with me and there is nothing I like better than a big bow for the bedroom valance. Why not choose a pretty flowered chintz for drapery panels and valance? Tie back the drapery panels with bows, too. And for a totally coordinated bedroom look, buy enough flowered chintz for quilted bedspread and headboard upholstery.

The bedroom for the married couple can go soft blue, royal blue, and white for an elegant look. Hang a crown valance the full length of your picture window. A scalloped bottom would be effective for the valance detail. Hang sheer, white undercurtains across the picture window; the dead-hung drapery panels should be tied back at the headboard.

Here's a bedroom with two picture windows—but only one has a view. Never cascade the window that has a view with heavy fabrics and overly deep valances, such as swags and jabots. Use light fabrics and, perhaps, a shirred chintz (blues, greens, reds, pinks, on a white ground) for valances. One window can become your bed backdrop—a very fresh and exciting treatment when the window curtains are the same fabric as the bedspread.

Any young lady or gentleman would enjoy this bedroom window wall when homework time arrives. The wall brackets and shelves are of the do-it-yourself variety. The desk, set at a right angle to the window, has a practical, laminated top. At the window hangs a shade in orange and white stripes. Actually, the shade is a do-it-yourself creation; the orange stripes were painted onto the shade using a mastic and spray paint procedure.

For those who don't like a bedroom headboard on an outside wall, the niche effect for the bedroom window wall is a good suggestion. A fabric-laminated shade is shown here; it coordinates with the wallpaper used within the niche itself. Coordinated wallpapers and fabrics are on the high priority list of decorators around the world. The niche frame of walnut was installed 42 inches from the window wall itself. (The standard twin-size bed is some 39 inches wide. Allowing for the niche and the front tieback draperies of royal blue, 42 inches were required for easy fitting.) Fabrics should be loosely hung.

This picture window highlights the city apartment for the modern man- or woman-about-town. The windows are treated with white, vinyl vertical blinds that can open and close easily and lend height to low, long, squatty windows.

Go Empire, in the style of Napoleon, for an elegant bedroom look. I like Empire-style draperies of rich, white silk trimmed, lined, and tied back with emerald green. Complement those Empire hangings with an Empire-style canopy for the bed!

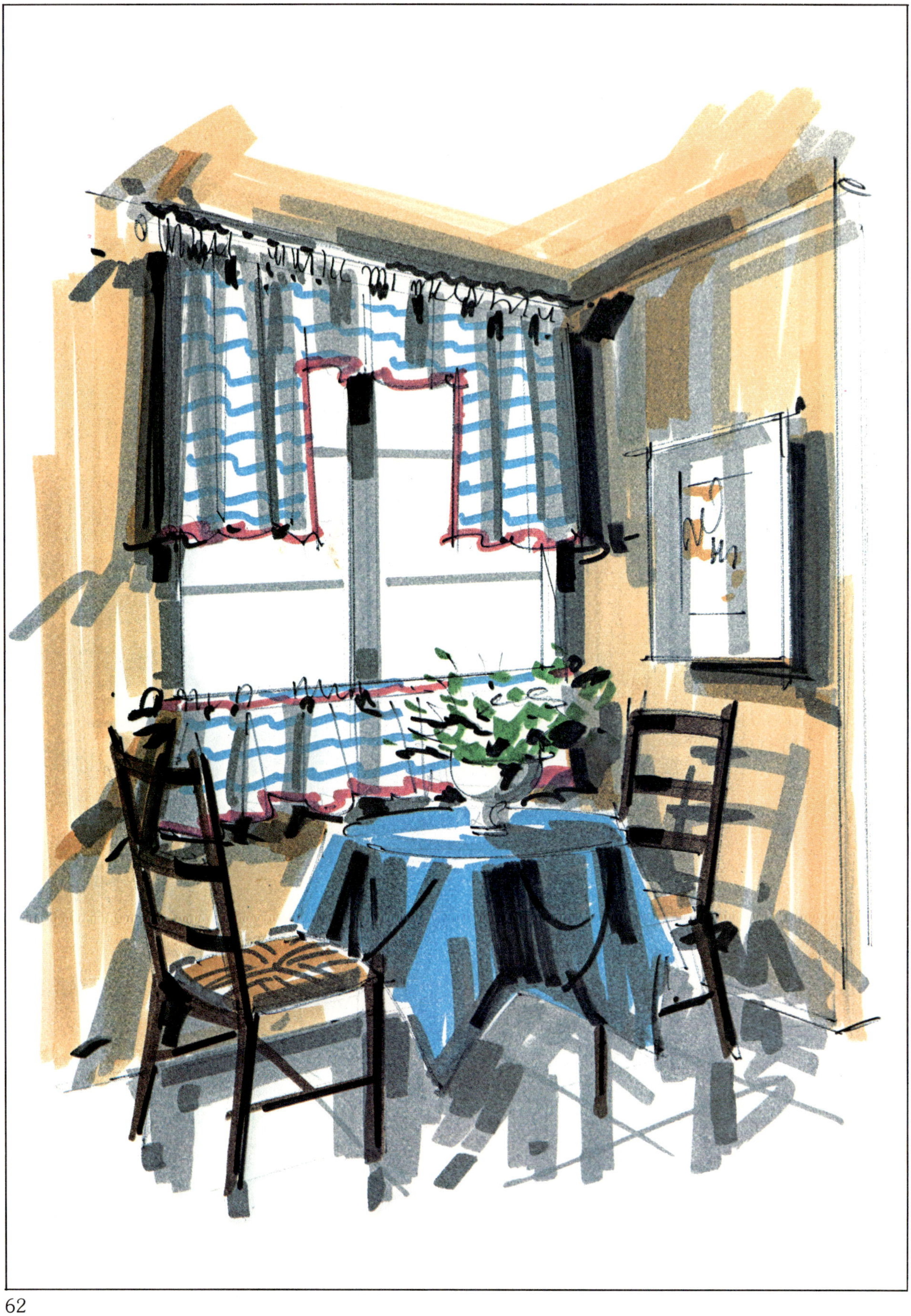

Chapter 3

Kitchen and Dining Room Window Treatments

Who enjoys cooking—or eating—in dark, dreary surroundings? Not me! Everybody loves cheery kitchens; cozy, happy-looking dining nooks; and restful, appetizing dining rooms. The kitchen is the place where many families gather first thing in the morning for fresh orange juice, crispy bacon, eggs—and, of course, that first eye-opening cup of coffee.

The kitchen with an adjoining dining nook is the place where many families gather for dinner at the end of the day to talk about the day's events. And the dining room is where the family does its entertaining, whether it be informal buffets or gracious small dinners for friends and neighbors.

Shouldn't your kitchen be filled with sunshine and light by day and with cozy warmth by night? But definitely! And that calls for window treatments that let in all that warm sunshine in the morning and still offer privacy at night.

Your dining nook should be a cheerful, comfortable area that serves double-duty after mealtime as a study center or a place where family projects can be completed. That calls for window treatments that inspire creative thinking and promote family togetherness.

Your dining room must also reflect and enhance those meals you've prepared so lovingly in that cheery kitchen, right down to coordinated window and table treatments.

I'm a fan of cafe curtains for kitchens and dining nooks. A gentle tug will pull them open to let in the morning light and an easy flick of the wrist will close them for privacy. I'm all for ruffled Priscillas, too, when you want a block for sunlight that's a bit too strong.

This valance with side panels is made from one piece of fabric. The blue and white check is trimmed in vibrant red. The low window curtains, made of the same blue and white check and trimmed in red, are hung on a pole. *(Left)*

For the dining room, I like curtains and draperies that give the illusion of space and serenity at night and that mix comfortably with your table linens, silver, and china. And if you want to go modern in your dining room, vertical blinds that have been color-coordinated to walls and table are an appetizing choice. Floor-to-ceiling louvers can block a bad view in a dining room, and floor-to-ceiling screens can be faced in fabric or paper to unify all your dining room elements.

What about those poor folk who have no warm sunshine to brighten their kitchens and dining nooks? City dwellers know all too well about the kitchen window that faces a gloomy gray airshaft or dining nook windows that look out on a boring brick wall. Well, I have an answer for them: It's no secret that I'm all for bright, happy colors—lemon yellow, tangy orange, tomato red, sky blue—for kitchen window treatments. They work well in dining nooks, too, especially dark ones. In the pages that follow, you'll see how color at windows can shed light on even the most dungeonlike kitchens and dining nooks. You will see how coordinating window shades and curtains can give pizazz to undistinguished windows. And you will see how imaginative graphics that you can create yourself and apply to window treatments can add that necessary Tabasco flavor to a meal-centered room.

You will see on the pages that follow a great mixture of formal and informal window decorations. I believe in going light and informal for kitchens and dining nooks; save those swags and jabots for the dining room. Kitchens and dining nooks should be kept warm, inviting, and simple. Dining rooms can go casual or formal, traditional or way-out modern.

One of the nicest things about simple kitchen and dining nook window treatments is the ease with which they can be changed. And, unless you really go all out with period window decoration in the dining room, this same advantage can apply there, too. After all, you can't change your silver and china patterns every season! Changing appliances and built-in cabinets in the kitchen is also a once-in-a-lifetime proposition for most families. But at least you're not stuck with your window treatments! You may hate your ten-year-old refrigerator, but you can still go wild at your windows. You may rue the day that your bridal consultant talked you into that silver pattern, but, for pennies, the dead-hung panels at your dining room windows can be changed to give your lovely room a touch of spring or fall.

Because kitchen and dining nook window treatments are usually done in cottons or other inexpensive washables, it's easy to change off when the mood strikes you. If you have red gingham venetian blinds at your kitchen windows and cafe curtains of red gingham in the dining nook, why not take down those gingham curtains from time-to-time and replace them with cafes of tiny red, white, and green flowers or red and white ticking stripes, or sheer white cafe curtains? Cafe curtains are easy and inexpensive to make; you can have several pairs and change off frequently.

In the dining room, translucent sheers of a neutral color can be framed with dead-hung panels that are changeable to match placemats and tablecloths. If your cooking and eating rooms have no view, you might like to use screens with fabric inserts at the windows. Those fabric inserts can be changed with the seasons, too. Your rooms may be dark and cheerless, but the season will come alive in your window treatments.

If you don't want to go the curtain way in kitchen and dining room windows, there are many attractive alternatives, such as laminated shades, louver shutters, and beads.

You can create a space-age window treatment with venetian blinds of sparkling, polished aluminum or with beads of shiny, silvery metal. Even city kitchen windows can be country fresh with white louver shutters below and shelves for green plants above. Your kitchen, dining nook, or dining room can hint of the tropics with white, roll-up, bamboo blinds and cafe curtains of a palm-tree design. Or, maybe your decorating tastes prefer the Mediterranean. This might call for dark wood solid panel shutters against white stucco walls.

In this brief chapter introduction, I have tried to indicate the importance of window treatments in your food-centered rooms. Their value in regulating the light, in setting a seasonal mood, and in setting a style—whether that style is country rustic, city slicker, or foreign and exotic—cannot be underestimated.

I have also tried to indicate how curtains, screens, shutters, and beads in bright, happy colors can work miracles, even in a dark kitchen or dining room. A new kitchen window treatment may not turn you into Julia Child, nor will it make dishwashing fun; a new set of dining nook curtains probably won't inspire a balky youngster to eat his spinach; and a bold, exotic treatment for your dining room windows won't get rid of The Man Who Came to Dinner. But, believe me, when it comes to peaceful preparation and enjoyment of meals for you and your family, zippy new window treatments can work miracles!

Make a three-sided frame for your dining room windows. Cover the frame with a floral-designed wallpaper border. Use the border wallpaper for a crown molding detail. Within the framework of the created pelmet, hang undercurtains of white silk. You can create the patterned floral look around your room solely with wallpaper borders.

When redecorating your dining room, why not paint the walls and woodwork white? At your windows, hang draperies and valances of hydrangea blue silk. Trim the draperies and valances in green to match the upholstery of the seats of your dining chairs. You can tie back draperies very high in the Regency style to reveal those soft, white, silky undercurtains.

Organdy criss-cross curtains can be used in the modern kitchen. This room combines white plastic-laminated kitchen cabinets, trimmed in apple green, with a Spanish terra-cotta tile floor and ruffled, bordered organdy curtains for a young and unified look. *(Left)*

Those gorgeous windows with the stained-glass look should definitely not be relegated to cathedrals! You can create a stained-glass window decor in your own kitchen simply by installing a recently fabricated panel that fits directly in front of your picture window. The panel can be hinged directly to existing window frames, allowing you to open the panel and wash the clear glass behind it. A less-expensive way of achieving the stained-glass look and one that children will enjoy is to apply colored acetates with black masking tape "leading." *(Right)*

Wondering what to do with the window over the kitchen sink? Choose a woven shade! In the shade, use the colors from your kitchen counters, cabinets, floor, and appliances.

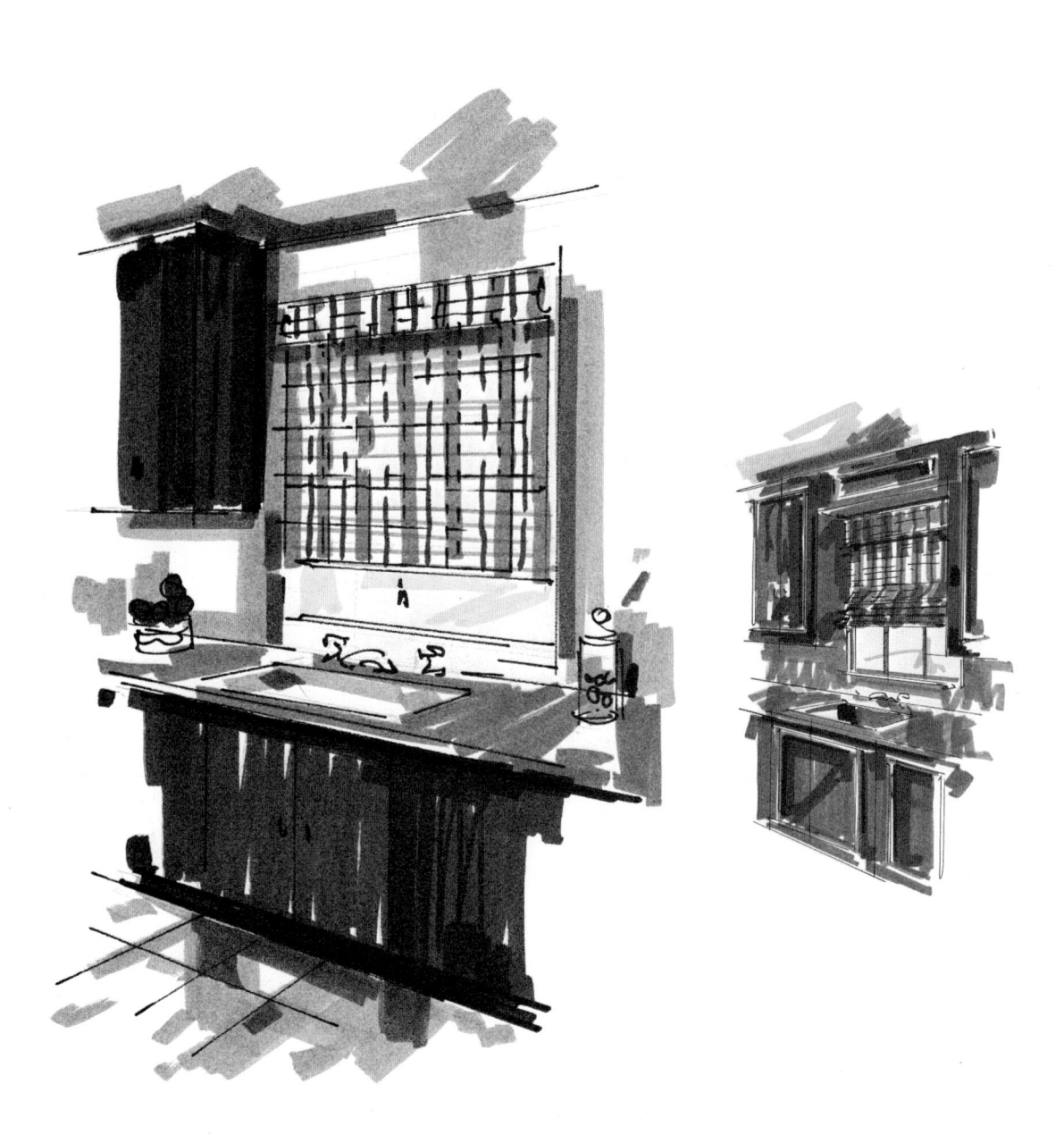

For kitchen windows where window panes open out, try a shaped, three-sided frame pelmet of plywood, covered in a snappy new plaid design. The frame in the illustration was used at open-out windows. The fabric cover-up for the plywood is a plaid of purples, pinks, greens, and yellows on a mint green background.

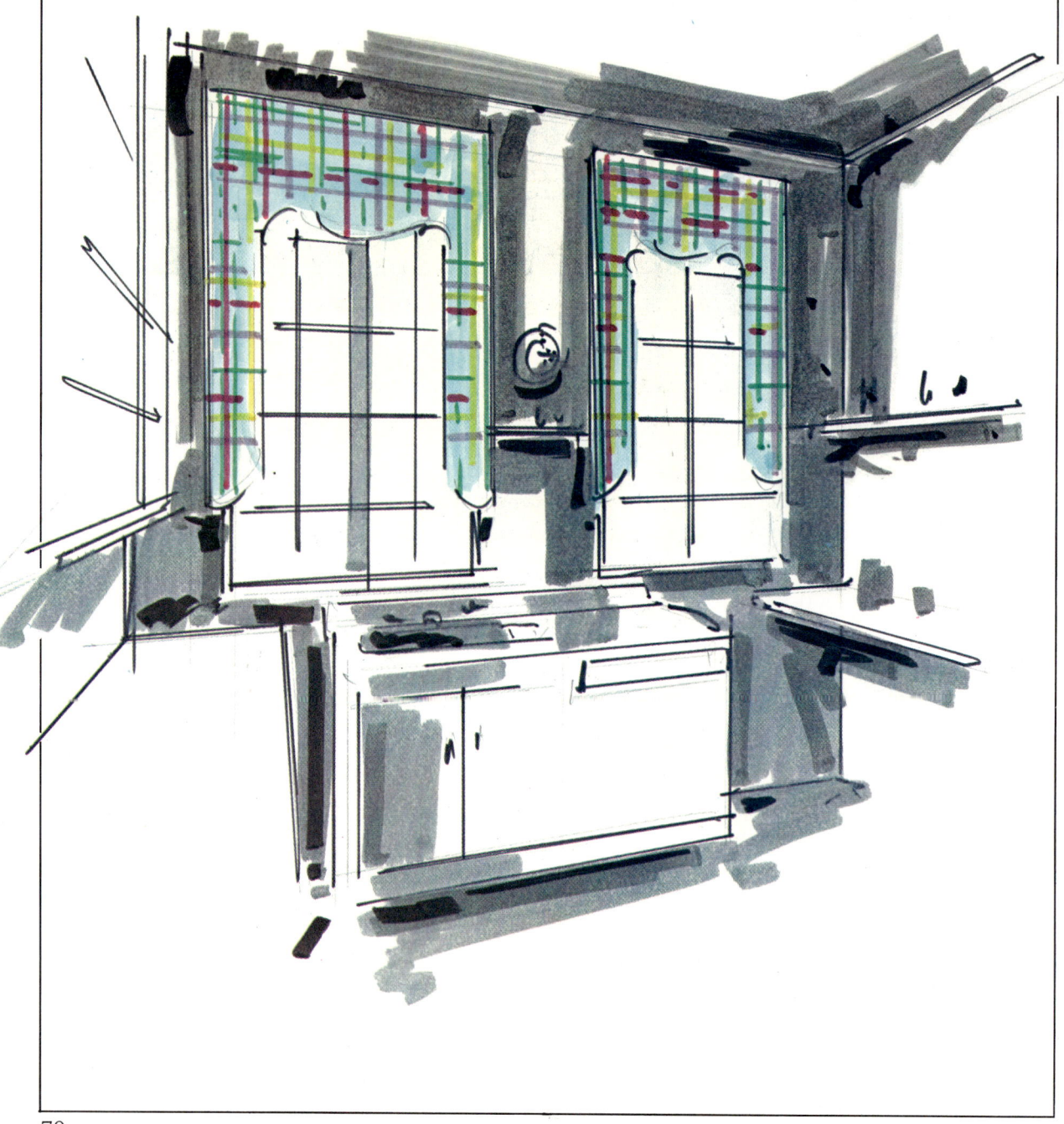

The ugly window in the living room–dining room combination can be hidden if you install a curved valance frame, as illustrated, to create a casual, comfortable dining room alcove. Doesn't everybody enjoy a corner table? A curved shape is almost always preferred to a straight form. To let the light inside, the window area has tied-back drapery under an Empire valance. The white sheers are hung from a curved track.

The window shade in the kitchen should be tangy and zippy. Who needs window curtains in the kitchen anyway? This kitchen, with a wallpapered ceiling and cutout and plywood valance covered with the same paper, features an orange shade. *(Left)*

Supergraphics can work with the Mediterranean look. Here, the terra-cotta tile color is picked up in the window shade design, which carries onto the ceiling. *(Right)*

Have you ever considered making a window drapery of industrial chain? You can buy the chain in zinc or anodized brass colors. The chain comes on rollers and can be cut exactly to the dimension of your window; the chain strings can be hung on an ordinary traverse curtain rod. In a modern kitchen, like this one with its white and stainless look, I've hung silvery metal chains. *Left)*

For a garden look without draperies, how about a window full of plants? Shelves made of glass or acrylic can be installed in window casings, or you can build a freestanding shelf arrangement in front of the window. *(Right)*

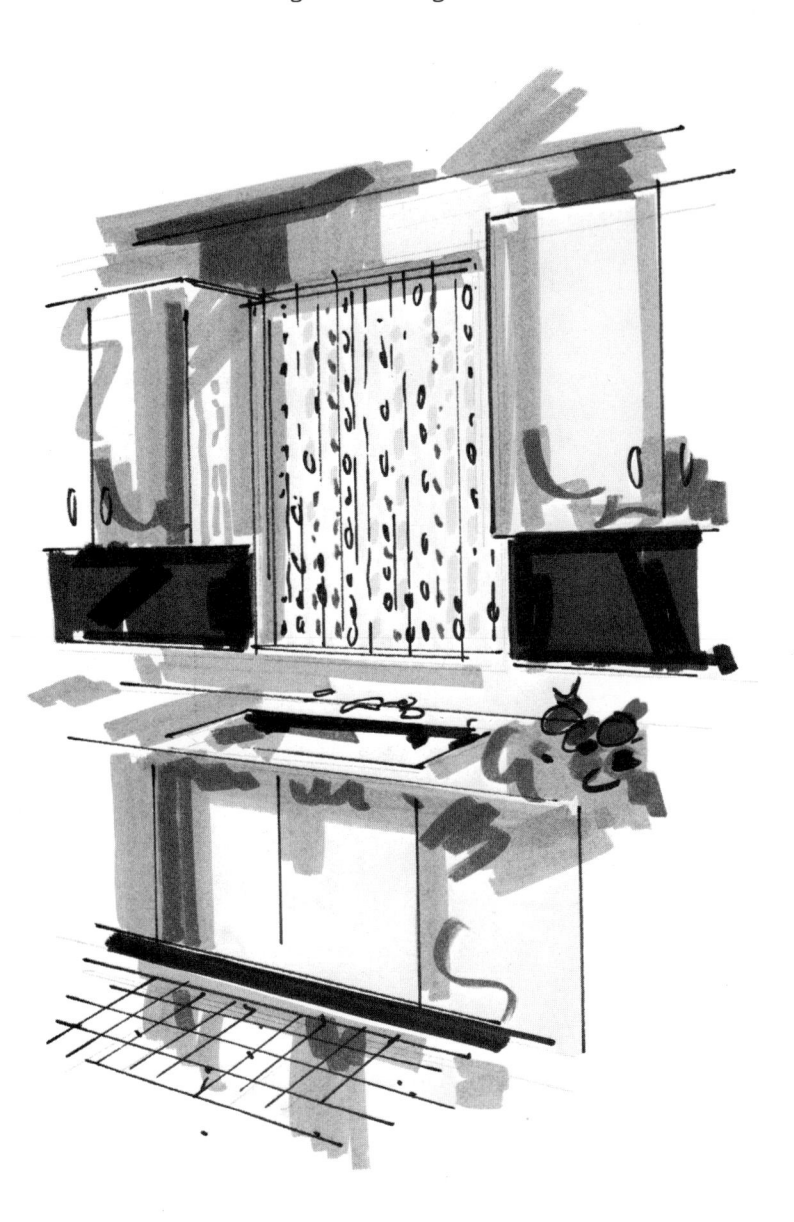

For the very classic at heart, what about a window wall in the dining room, set with columns at each side and a center window design of white Austrian shades? Naturally, I'd like to see that dining room with a white marble floor, a bronze and crystal chandelier, gold framed dining chairs with gold velvet upholstered seats, and, for the *pièce de résistance*, a gold double-pedestal-base table with a white marble top. Dinner guests in such a room will think they're dining at Versailles!

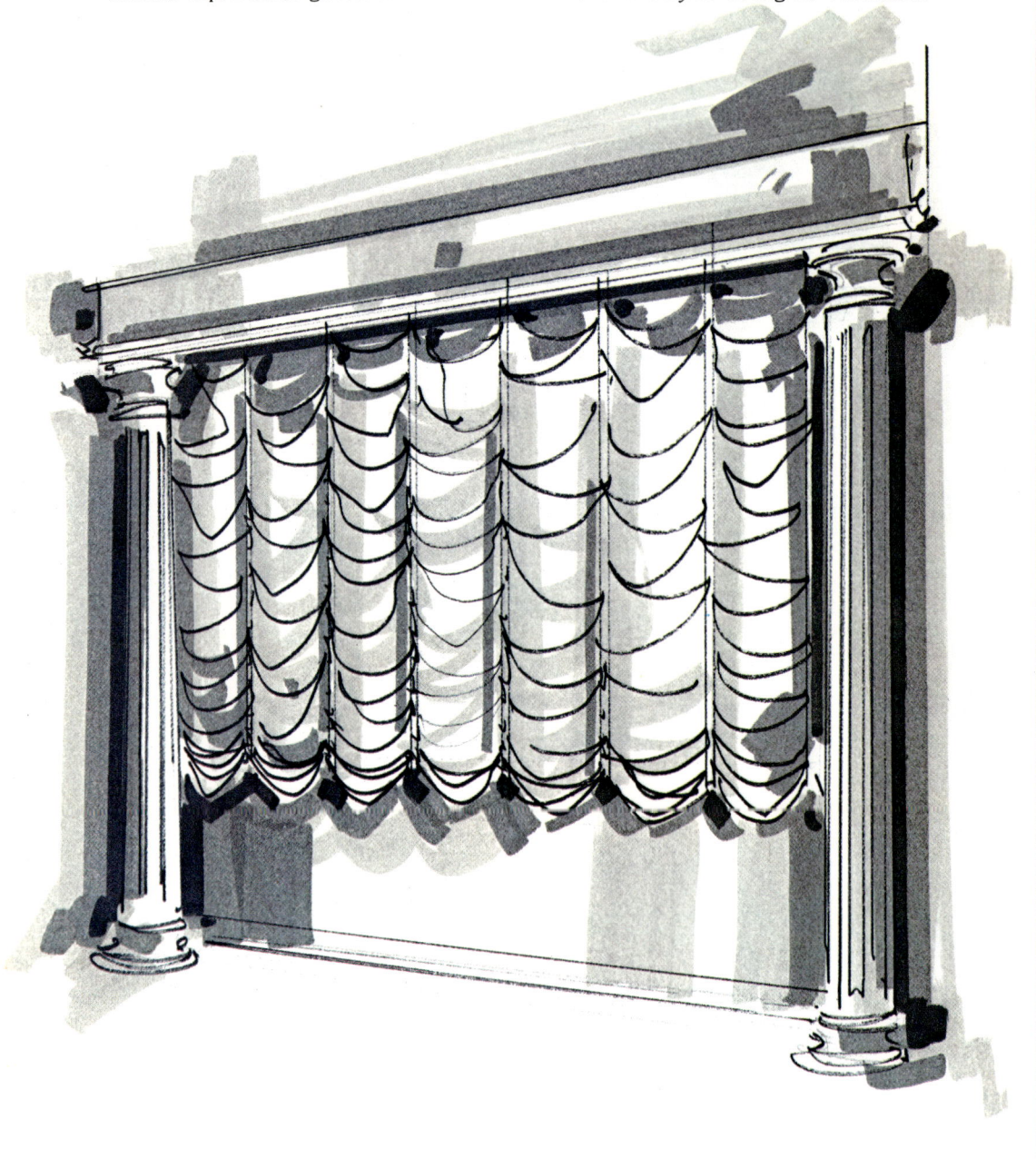

A soffit and side panels, created with plywood board that is trimmed with half-round molding, give this window a formal, yet casual look. The molding makes the look formal, and the green-painted trim provides the informality.

Austrian shades—the British call them "festoon blinds"—of sheer fabrics diffuse light most handsomely in a formal dining room, and they're oh, so elegant at night! Austrians can also cover up all those busy window mullions. I have used Austrian shades across full walls in dining room decorating to create a formal feeling. But Austrians can be informal, too! Try an Austrian shade of a yellow and green daisy print in your dining nook, or of a gay floral print in your kitchen. *(Below)*

I don't believe, ever, in trying to drape the window portion of your kitchen door exactly as you do the straightforward kitchen windows. Windows in doors require special attention. Here are six of my favorite treatments for them. *(Right)*

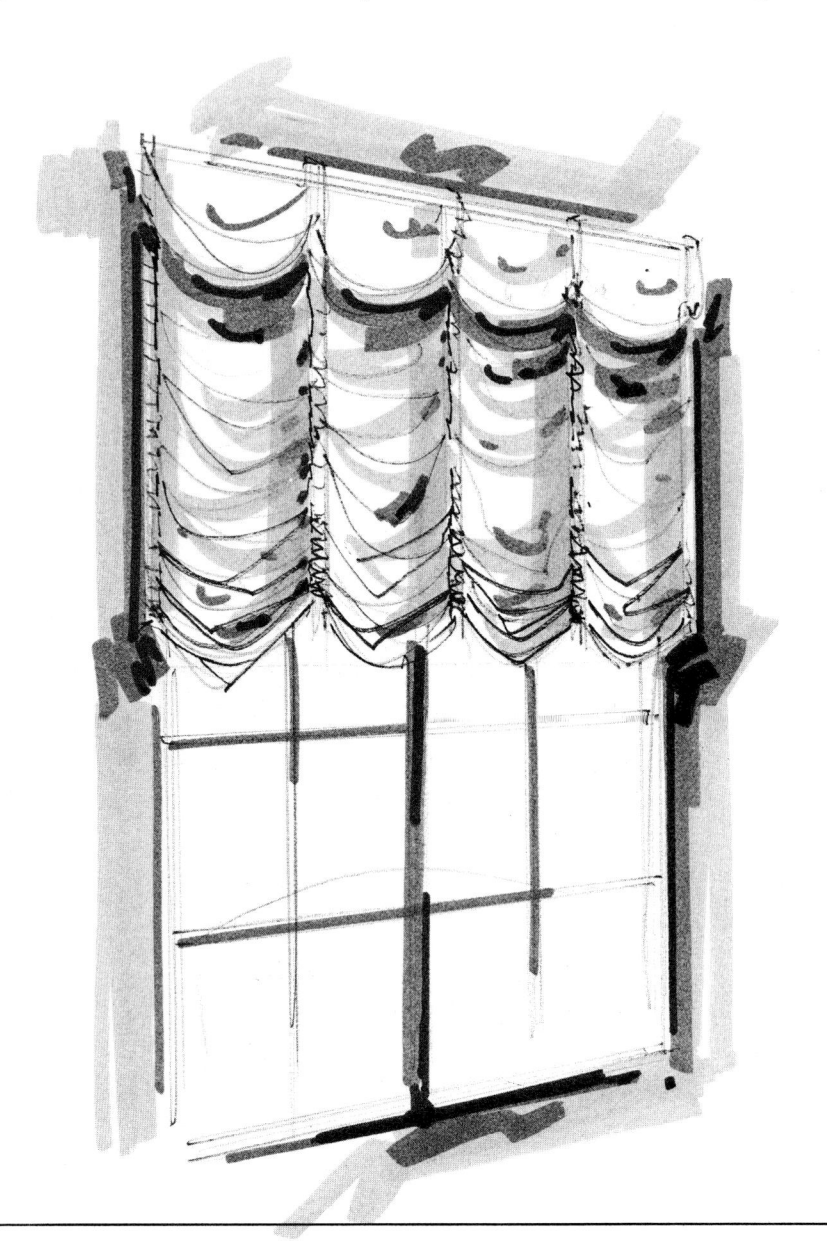

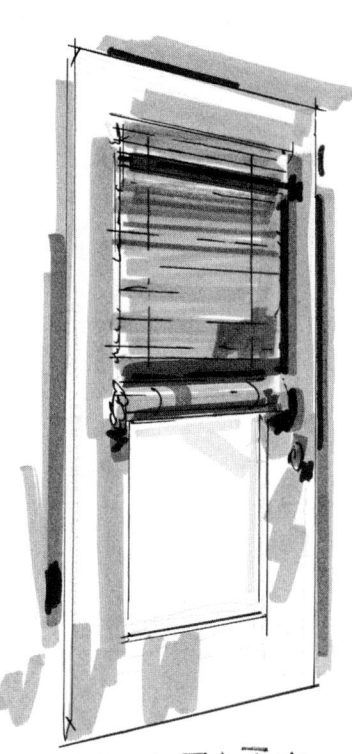

THE MATCHSTICK
BLIND - ON PULL
UP ROLLER

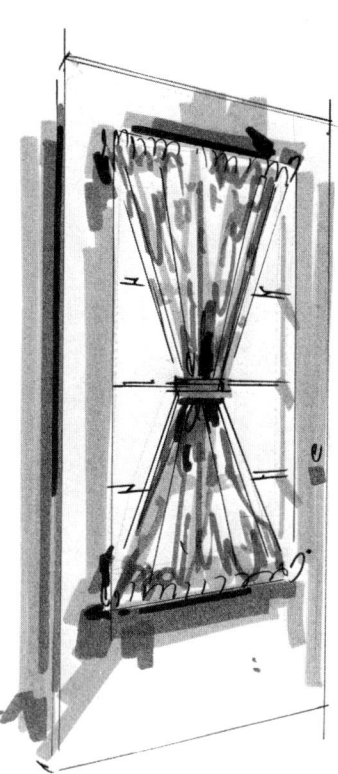

THE NIPPED-IN
CURTAIN

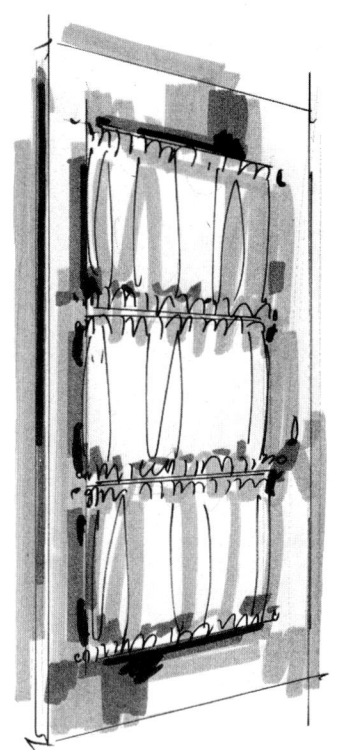

3 TIERS OF GATHERED
SHEERS

THE LAMINATED
ROLLER SHADE

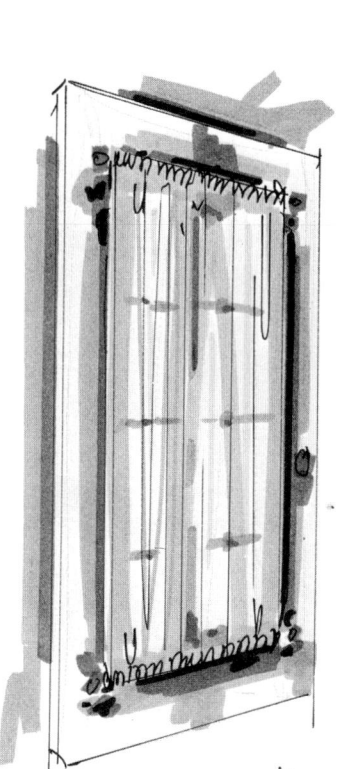

SHEERS - USING
THE ROD TOP AND
BOTTOM INSTALLATION

THE CAFE WRAP - ON
NARROW ROUND POLE

Some people install air-conditioning units in the upper portion of the kitchen window. Here, a reverse procedure of louver and cafe installation exists. The upper section, where the air conditioner rests, is covered by white louver shutters, while the lower window section is decorated with cafe curtains, done in a happy print.

In this instance, cafe curtains could have been used at both heights. When the air conditioner is in operation, naturally, the upper cafes must be opened. *(Left)*

Give your kitchen a fresh, country look with the newest in venetian blinds—gingham. Gingham blinds come in red, blue, emerald green, brown, and yellow. When used with a matching wallpaper and wood accents, gingham blinds will give even a city kitchen a country farmhouse flavor. *(Right)*

Vertical blinds, once thought of only for glass office buildings, are terrific in a modern dining room. Vertical blinds of vinyl fabric and of the woven materials can give your windows lots of pizazz, as well as height. I like the vinyl variety for ease of cleaning.

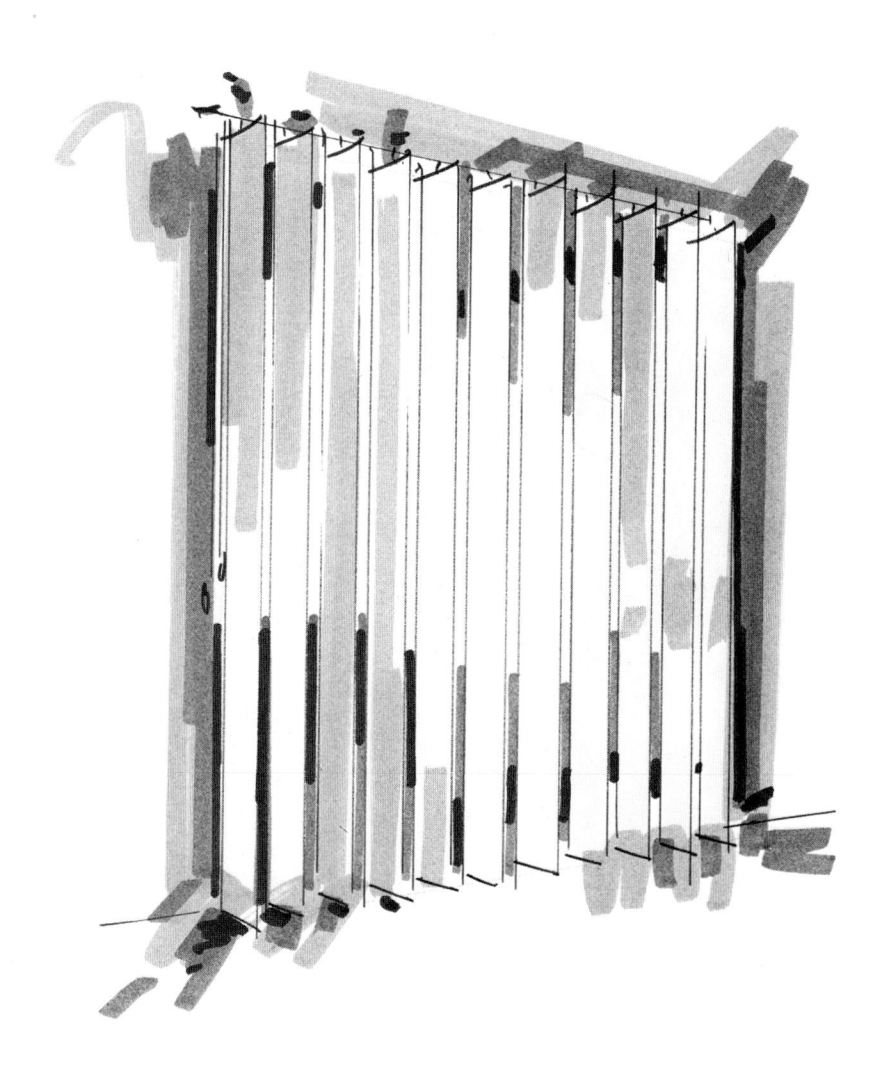

I like corner windows treated with shades (drapery can be used, too, of course). Here, white-duck Roman shades create a cozy, yet open, look in the dining nook. Who wouldn't enjoy such a charming view while sipping a cup of morning tea?

Bottoms up with window shades! The shade rises from the floor to hide the air conditioner in this bedroom. A frame of 1 × 12 board has been installed here, to which the pull-down and pull-up shades have been attached.

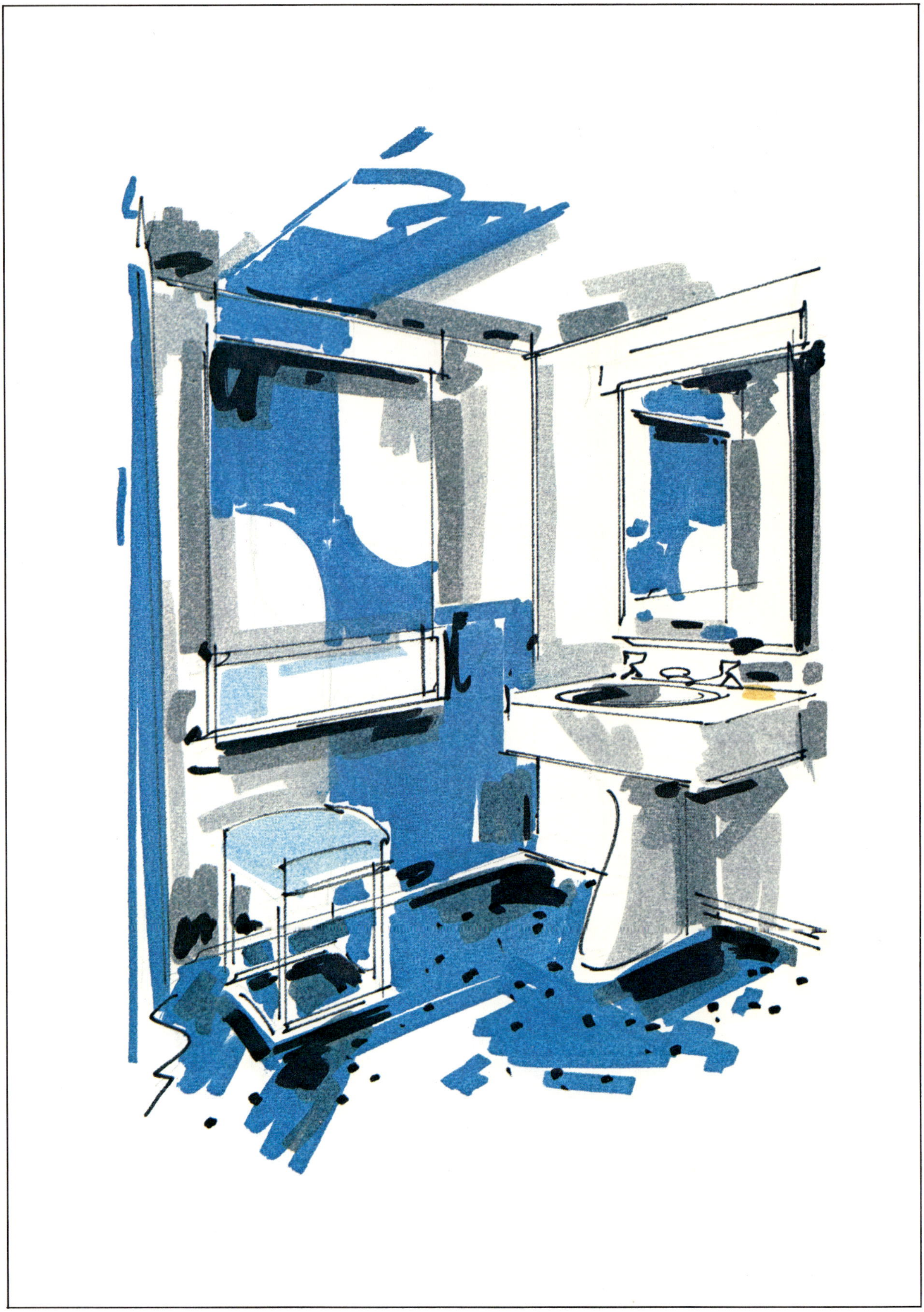

Chapter 4

Bathroom Window Treatments

Oh, those bathroom windows. They're the least-inspiring windows in any home, probably because they're often small and badly placed. But that's no reason to overlook them in your decorating scheme. Quite the contrary. Bathroom windows, especially, cry out to be dressed up. They need all the help they can get!

The "curtain way" is one way to dress up bathroom windows, but there are many other happy solutions: beads, screens, shutters, laminated shades, attractive venetian blinds, and many more. All can have their place in a bathroom.

Because bathrooms usually come outfitted with tile and fixtures not selected by the occupants of the house, you have to plan your windows around a set of "givens." In fact, the window treatments in your bathroom may be one of the few ways you'll have to dress up your bathroom's appearance.

If your bathroom has drab, gray tile and dark burgundy trim, add some punch with printed vinyl wallcovering of silver, burgundy, and pink, and dress up the windows with thin-slat venetian blinds of silvery metal. If you have pink tiles in your bath and you long for a tailored look, why not add a window shade and paint it with a bold geometric graphic of navy blue and pink? It makes a sophisticated antidote to prissy pink, especially when teamed with navy patent vinyl wallcovering. Navy blue and pink towels and a navy blue carpet will complete the picture attractively.

For privacy and pep in the bathroom, paint a bold graphic on a white, room-darkening shade. *(Left)*

Perhaps you're wondering how you can make your twentieth-century bathroom fit the Victorian decor you've chosen for the rest of your home. I had a friend with that dilemma. She solved it by locating an old panel of stained glass in an antique shop. By suspending that panel of pretty vivid glass from the ceiling in front of her window, she found the privacy she needed and the antique look she wanted.

If the bathroom is the place where you love to primp and preen for hours on end, you may want a truly pretty bath. Ruffled sheer curtains dress up a bathroom beautifully; and for privacy, hang those ruffled sheers over a window shade and laminate it in a floral fabric to match the wallcovering.

Or, maybe your bath has to serve another, less-glamorous function. It may be the place where you give the children those unwelcome rinsings. You may want a bathroom that's all practicality and bright, cheery color. Bright colors, in my opinion, always make those unpleasant chores a bit more bearable. How about louver shutters in a zippy color—tomato red or emerald green—for your bath? Or why not give your bathroom a touch of the great outdoors with rows of plants growing happily on shelves of lucite in that humid bathroom window?

When you think "window decorating," don't overlook your little bathroom window. It may be small and tucked away, but the right window treatment for it might make the difference in your bathroom.

The bathroom window is the perfect place for a garden—provided that you choose the plants wisely. Certain varieties love moisture and they're right at home in a steamy bathroom environment. Put up lucite shelves in the window (they're nice and airy-looking), and cover the walls with a lush, palm-tree design vinyl to round out the jungle paradise look!

Warm browns and beiges enrich this bachelor pad bath. Tailored bamboo roller blinds at the windows blend in well with the wooden louvered cabinetry under the sink.

Floral vinyl wallcovering and ruffly sheer Priscilla curtains at the window make this bathroom a pretty place in which to primp.

For a children's bathroom, why not apply a geometric design to the shades—one of a girl, the other of a boy. Cut out the boy and girl figures from brown paper. Apply them, using double-faced tape, to the white window shade and paint the whole shade black. When the paint has dried, remove the two brown paper cutouts and—eureka!—your happy figures will pop right out in white.

A floor-to-ceiling bathroom window with a pretty patio view needs no window treatment at all, providing the patio is private, of course. To make that window the star of the room, sheet-mirror the wall next to it to reflect the lush patio greenery outside.

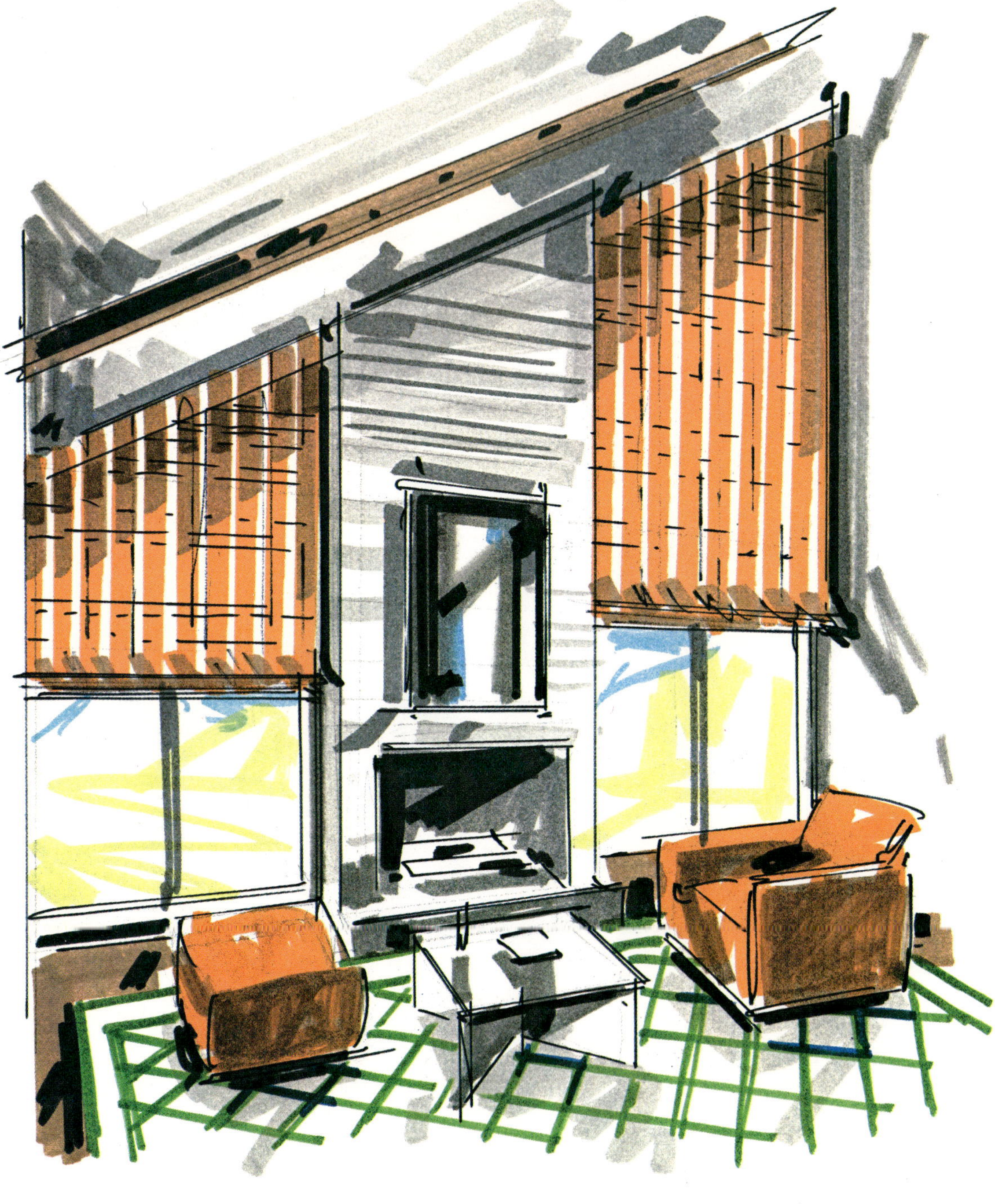

Chapter 5

Special or Problem Window Treatments

I've discovered that special windows, whether they're Palladian framed arches in a Georgian mansion or the trapezoidal paned windows of a woodsy country home, are often *the* architectural feature that convinces a family, once and for all, that "this is the house for us!"

Take, for example, that super floor-to-ceiling wall of sliding glass windows where a family can sit and watch the changing seasons. Who can put a price on the pure pleasure such a window brings to everyone in the family?

Or take that pair of dormer windows in the children's bedroom. They offer the perfect set-up for a young mother who wants two built-in areas for privacy and a special place for each child. And those majestic, modern, slanting windows that flank a fireplace and soar to the uppermost corners of a beamed cathedral ceiling offer another challenge. Without proper window accents for light and view, this room's most valuable feature would be wasted!

The bay window in the living room or family room, where father and son can enjoy a chess game without constant interruption, pays off, not only as a beautiful focal point for the room, but in peace of mind, as well. And the bay window in the master bedroom—with its soft and comfortable chairs—can become a haven of tranquillity for Mom and Dad. Or what about that window set into the top half of your kitchen door? Lucky you, to have that extra source of light, where, at a glance, you can keep a watchful eye on backyard activity.

Yes, all those special windows are a plus!

Woven shades of the Roman style are one answer for those modern, slanted living room windows. Here, the windows on each side of a white brick fireplace are decorated with woven orange and beige Roman blinds for a coordinated look. When ordering window treatments for slanted windows, be sure to measure each window! Here, the two windows are of two different heights. *(Left)*

Then again, some special windows are downright, out-and-out problems. I was brought up on the old adage that only when you stop thinking of your problems as problems and start thinking of them as challenges can you begin to solve them!

I like to think of problem windows as challenges and I get a big kick out of meeting that challenge. If you have a window that faces onto *nothing*, I'll show you how to treat it with a variety of approaches that will screen it off, camouflage it, or make it look like a door to somewhere.

I'll show you how to treat those problem windows that bulge with unsightly, but necessary, air conditioners with lattices or with combinations of shades and curtains that integrate the air conditioner with the rest of the room. Compared to the cost of custom carpentry, you can do it all yourself for practically nothing.

And those "ugly duckling" windows that don't match because of differences in height, width, or shape: I'll show you how—with valances, frames, or fabric—they can look as though they were made for each other.

So think of your special windows as the best expressions of taste and style you and your family can offer, whether you live in a mansion or a simple cabin in the woods. Think of your problem windows as challenges—and watch the creative ideas fly!

Don't cover your sunburst arch—let the sun shine in from the top. Here, tieback draperies to match the wallcovering are installed at the straight-top window mullion for an open, sunshine look.

Loved by many, loathed by others, the bay window—if located in an apartment high above a city, with views on all sides—can be a delight. When located in an apartment on a low floor, side-by-side with another bay window of the adjoining apartment, the bay window becomes a problem. This window is designed to frame a terrific view—San Francisco Bay!

For that light and airy look, frame the concrete soffit and sides of a bay window with a white-painted wooden lattice. Line the back of the lattice with canary yellow duck. Paint the ceiling of the bay (and the wall sections under the windows) canary yellow, too.

Treat a bay window, recessed under a concrete soffit, with a valance, overdraperies, and Roman window shades that are all of the same print. Attach the valance to your concrete soffit at the ceiling line. Hang draperies from the ceiling, too! Because the bay is a recessed architectural element, I would suggest lining the overdraperies and shirred valance with a happy color. Overdrapery panels, shown here, can be stationary; they need not draw.

If the windows of your bay window don't go to the floor, you can make them look as if they do. Paint the wall sections under your bay windows white and hang undercurtains of a white, washable, sheer fabric on a curved window curtain rod (curved traverse rods are available on today's market). To open and close the curtains, use baton pulls instead of a cord and pulley attachment. A shaped valance can be installed in front of the concrete soffit, along with overdraperies.

For those who have a bay window and want to give it a formal look, why not try an Imperial-styled valance? This bell-and-swag design should be installed on the concrete soffit. With the Imperial valance and matching overdraperies, treat the windows themselves with matching colored Austrian shades (with a matching color ruching on the shades).

Those people who have bay windows that go to the floor are lucky, indeed. For the formal lady (and formal drawing room), my favorite floor-to-ceiling bay window treatment calls for swags and jabot valances, complete with overdrapery to draw, and Austrian shades to raise and lower. Because the formal look requires soft, silky fabrics, how about a rich gold window treatment with swags that are lined in lemon yellow?

Make your bay windows an integral part of the room by installing tieback draperies of a print to match your room's wallpaper. Coordinating fabrics and wallpapers are available everywhere today, so don't hesitate to decorate a room in the one print that you love. But when you do, make sure all upholstered furniture is covered in the same print! White undercurtains in the bay can give your window—with or without a view—a soft feeling.

The dormer window, found in many an American home, can be most attractive. The dormer here is treated with louvers, to which upper and lower cafe curtains can be added (or a sheer curtain under a simple valance). *(Left)*

In this dormer window, two simple rows of cafe curtains are hung on poles, straight across the window. The window seat is covered in a coordinated fabric. *(Right)*

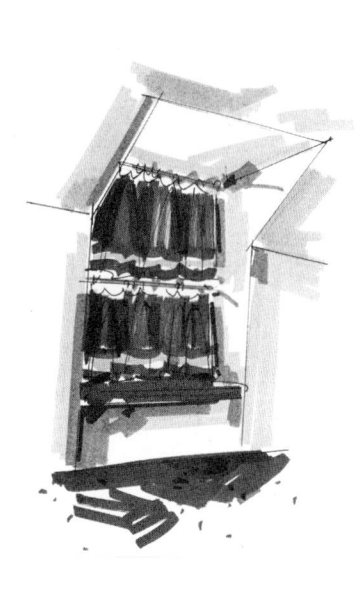

101

There are two kinds of skylights: the overhead type that is set in a flat roof and the slanted kind, shown here. Both types can be served by the same "constant tension" kind of installation, which works on cords that hold the shade firmly in place. These shades are functional as well. Unshaded overhead skylights can concentrate strong sunlight onto a portion of the room at certain times of day making it uncomfortable and hot.

The star attraction in this room is a pair of slanted skylight windows framed by stained wood beams. Bottom-up shades, which also do well on regular windows and overhead skylights, are the answer to windows where daylight needs to be muted, but never cut off, and where privacy is a must.

Here, soft ruffled curtains fall under a shaped valance, fitted snugly to the head of the dormer window. Fabric on the valance can match window seat cover, as shown, or it can coordinate with the rest of the fabric in the room. You can also paper or paint the valance, or stain it to accent the dormer angle. *Left)*

If you want to paint your dormer room, instead of following the complete papered look for walls and ceilings, consider making a feature of the architectural dormer. Paper it with a cheerful sky blue, emerald green, and yellow print on a white background. At the windows, use laminated shades of the fabric to match the wallpaper. The window bench seat can be covered in a fabric to match the window shade. If your dormer room is a bedroom, make sure that the bedspread and bedskirt are made of the same print! *(Right)*

If the dormer window in your upstairs bedroom has no window seat, why not hang draperies at the window that are made of a fabric to match the room's walls and ceiling? Here, a blue-on-white toile design for windows and walls coordinates the entire room.

Dramatize your windows with an arched valance—one that follows the contour of the window to a tee. This yellow valance, trimmed with green velvet braid, matches the pull-cord traverse rod installed over the draperies. If undercurtains are installed under the overdraperies, white sheers should be used so as not to destroy the line of the arched window. *(Left)*

In the modern dormer or barn dormer, why not louver shutters to the floor? Full-height louver shutters will make your dormer windows look higher. In this illustration, dormer walls have been painted the same color as the louver shutters—bright sunshine yellow! The walls in the dormer room are white and the beams are walnut. *(Right)*

A shirred sunburst is a very popular way to decorate the top of an arch. Fabric is tacked to the half-round form, gathered into the lower center, and detailed with a white, shirred rosebud. Curtains installed under the arch are of a melon and green flowery design on a white sheer ground. *(Left)*

Have you ever considered covering a sliding glass door-window with a drapery of industrial chain? You can buy the chain in zinc or anodized brass colors. The chain comes on rollers and can be cut exactly to the dimensions of your window. The chain strings can be hung on an ordinary traverse curtain rod. Bead, spool, or chain draperies draw as easily as regular window curtains. *(Right)*

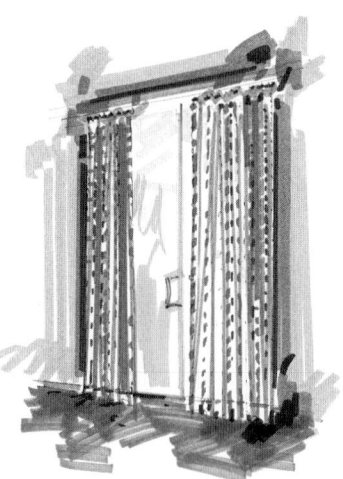

Many sliding glass door-windows should be left without a window decoration. Any window that overlooks a pool and gardens, sea, mountains, or just a simple rock garden ought to be left alone. The window decoration shown here is nature's own.

Chapter 6
A Picture Dictionary of Period Window Treatments

Period Window Treatments

Have you ever heard people talking about Regency drapery treatments? Or about Empire window effects? Have you ever wanted to create an elegant period look at the windows of your own home? I know that for many people, it's the rage. And I can understand their passion for the period look—it's elegant, it's luxurious, it's graceful. For windows, there's nothing quite as lush as those drapery treatments of yesteryear. We can all use a touch of luxury in our lives.

I have put together on the following pages a pictorial dictionary of period styles for windows. They are pretty; they are elegant; and any one of them could work well in the American home of today—provided that the room style is in keeping with the window treatment's period! Don't mix early English with Mediterranean decor, please. And don't throw together the look of Early American maple and pewter with an Empire window treatment.

That doesn't mean that you must use only antiques or reproductions in a room that features one of these period window treatments. Not at all! There are many contemporary and classic furniture styles—cube tables, Parsons tables, tuxedo sofas—that blend well with real period window treatments. All that mixing of contemporary and traditional is what's called the "eclectic" look, which is very much with us these days. Personally, I'm all for it!

So, whether you're the eclectic type or a period purist, use the pictorial period dictionary that follows as your guide to period windows with a punch.

Renaissance-

Renaissance-

Renaissance

Renaissance

Louis XIV

Louis XIV

Queen Anne

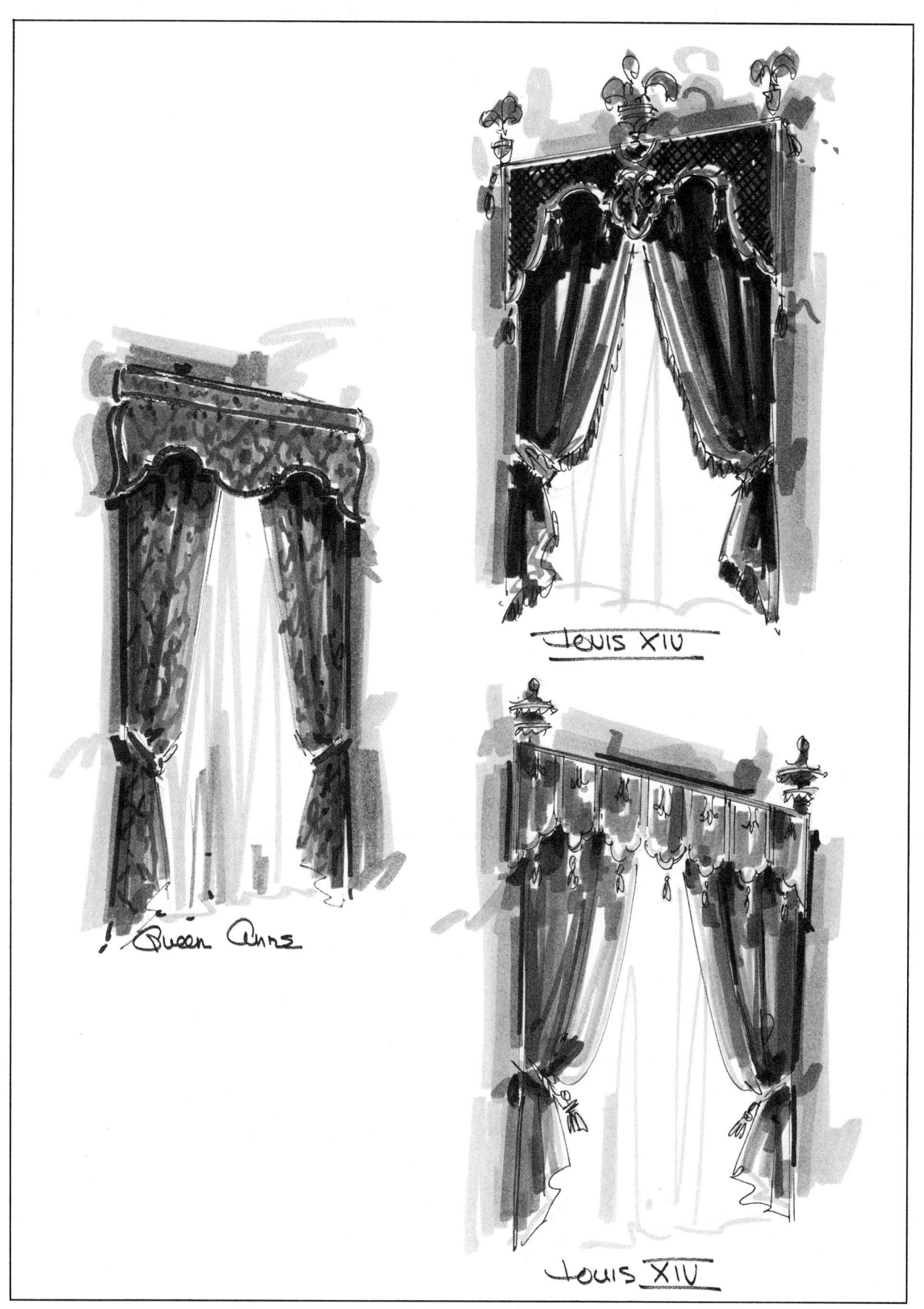

Louis XIV

Louis XIV

DIRECTOIRE

DIRECTOIRE

ADAM

Early Chippendale

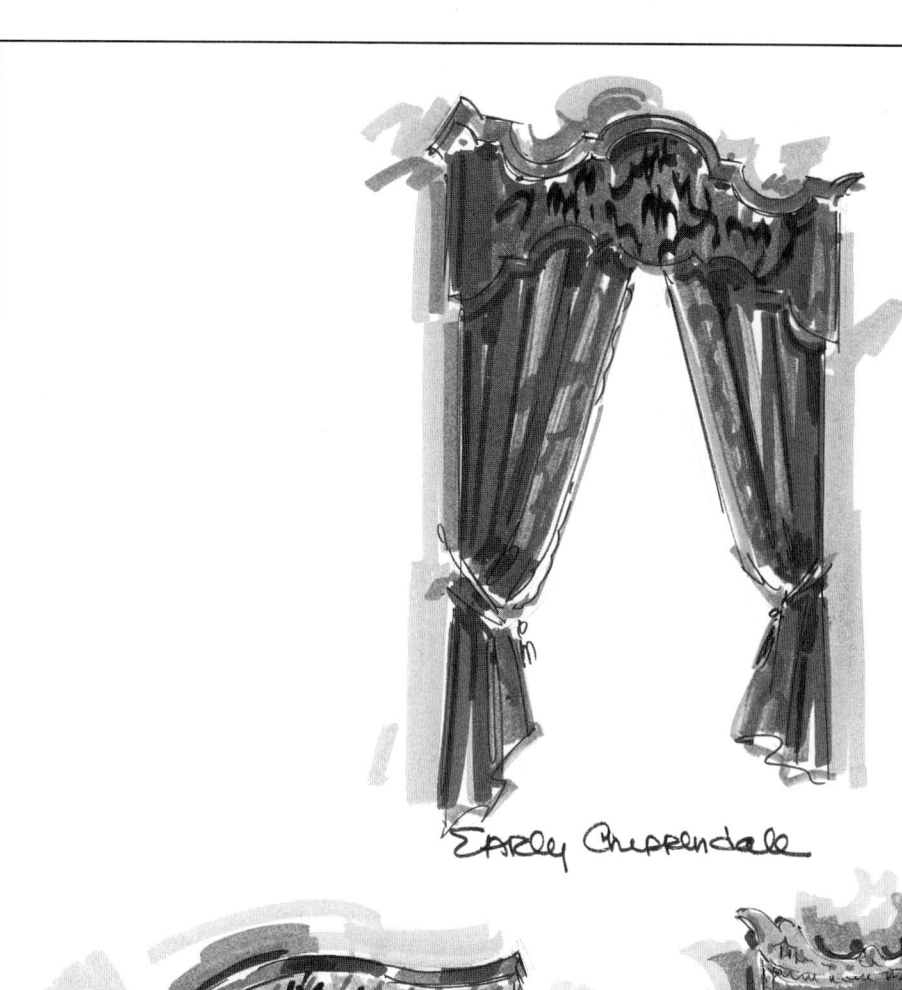

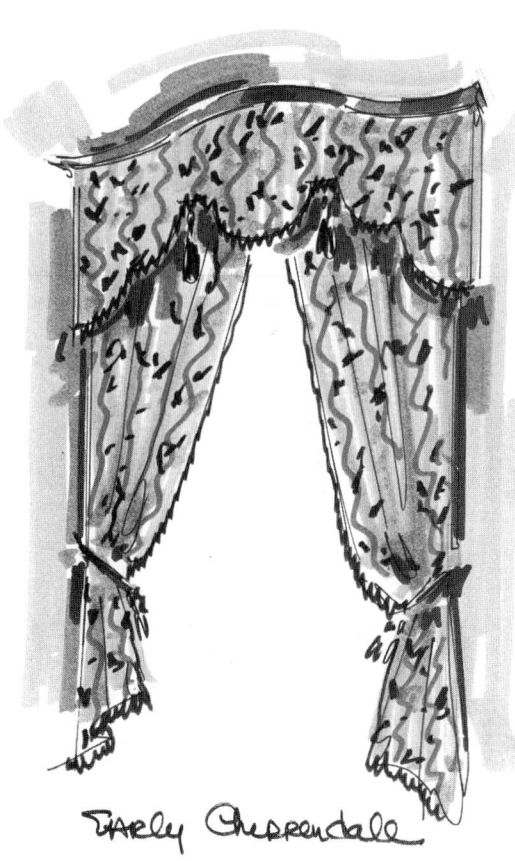

Early Chippendale

Chippendale

Louis XV

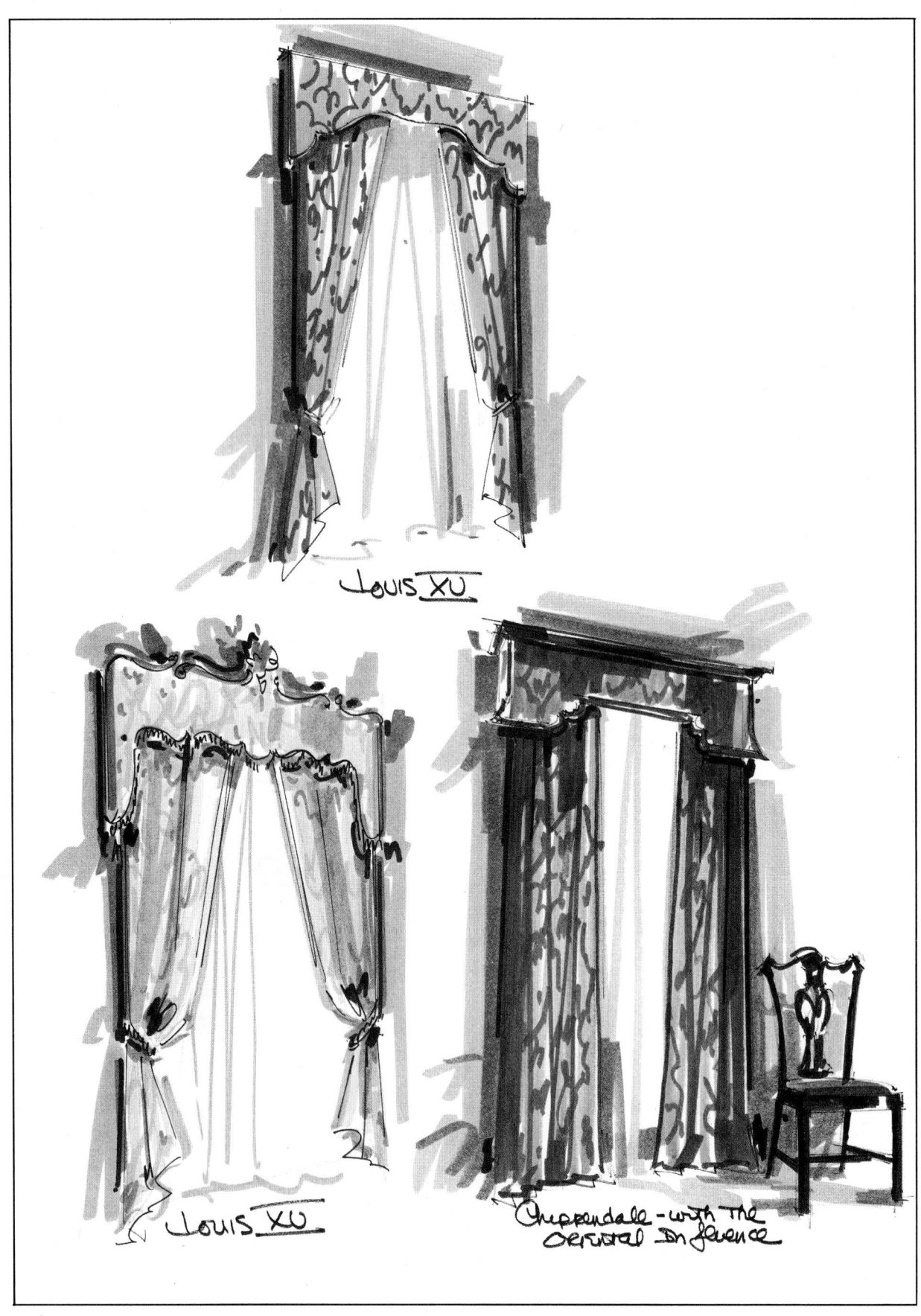

Louis XV

Chippendale – with the
Oriental Influence

Louis XV

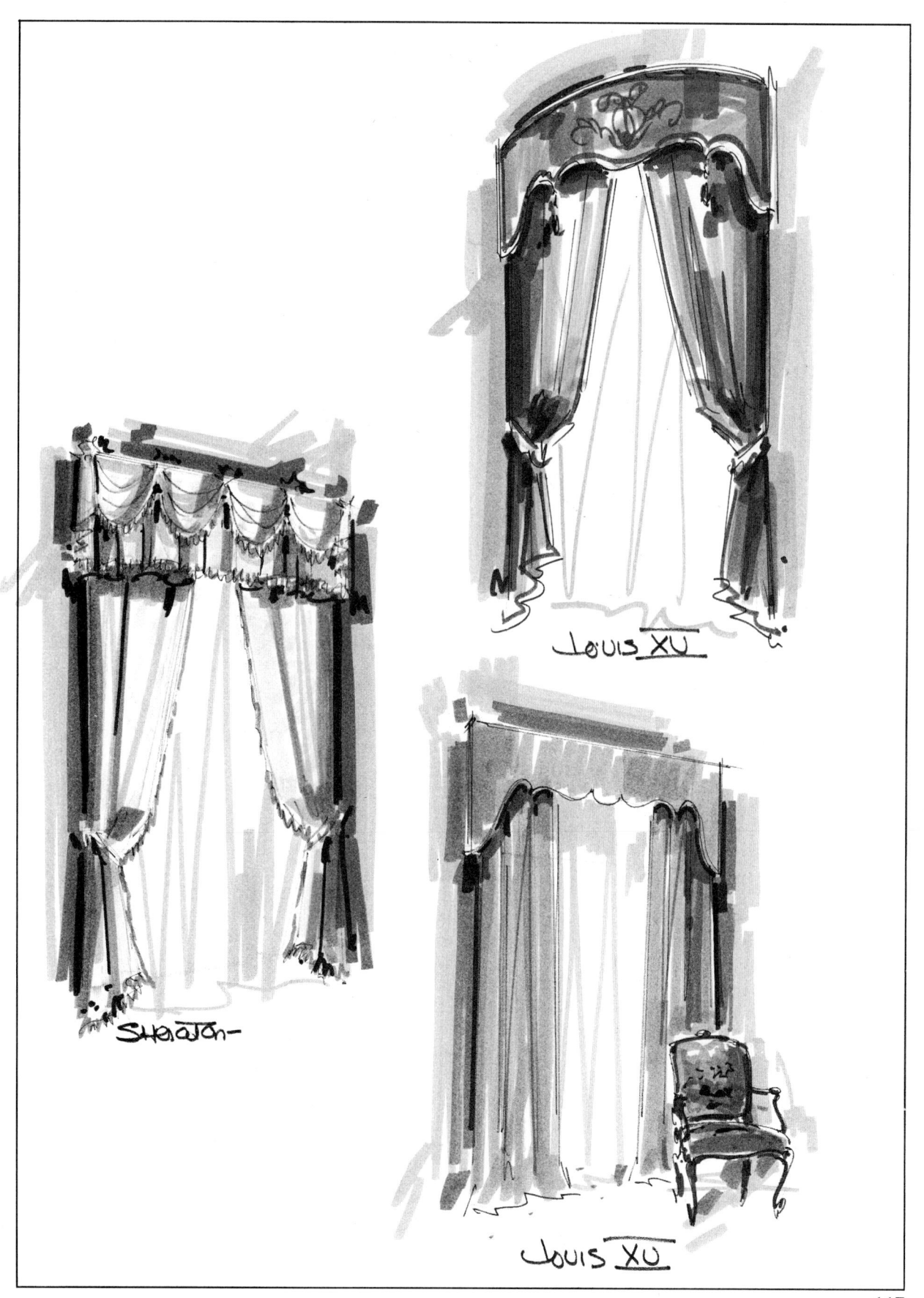

Sheraton

Louis XV

Régence

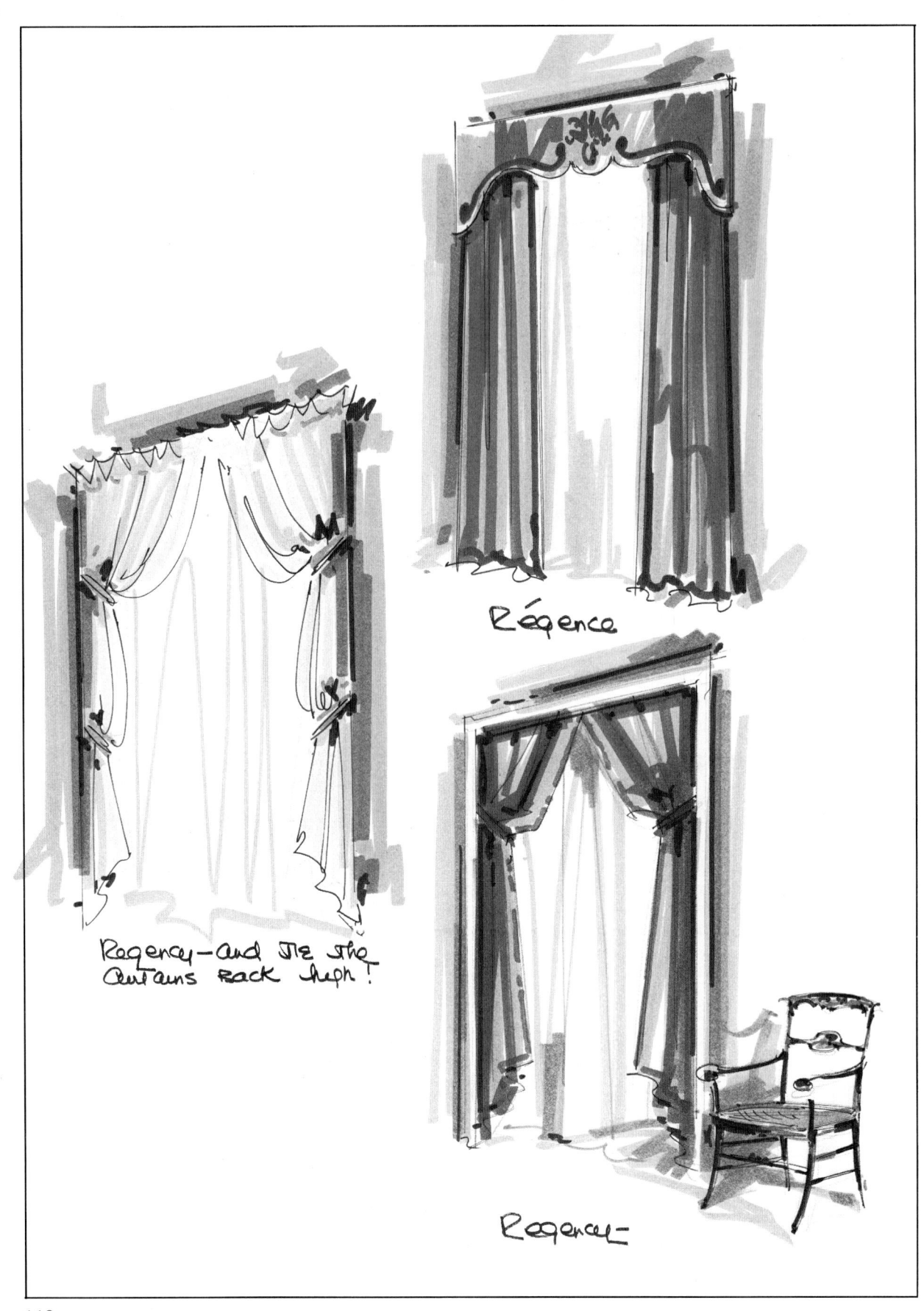

Regency — and tie the curtains back high!

Regency —

Régence

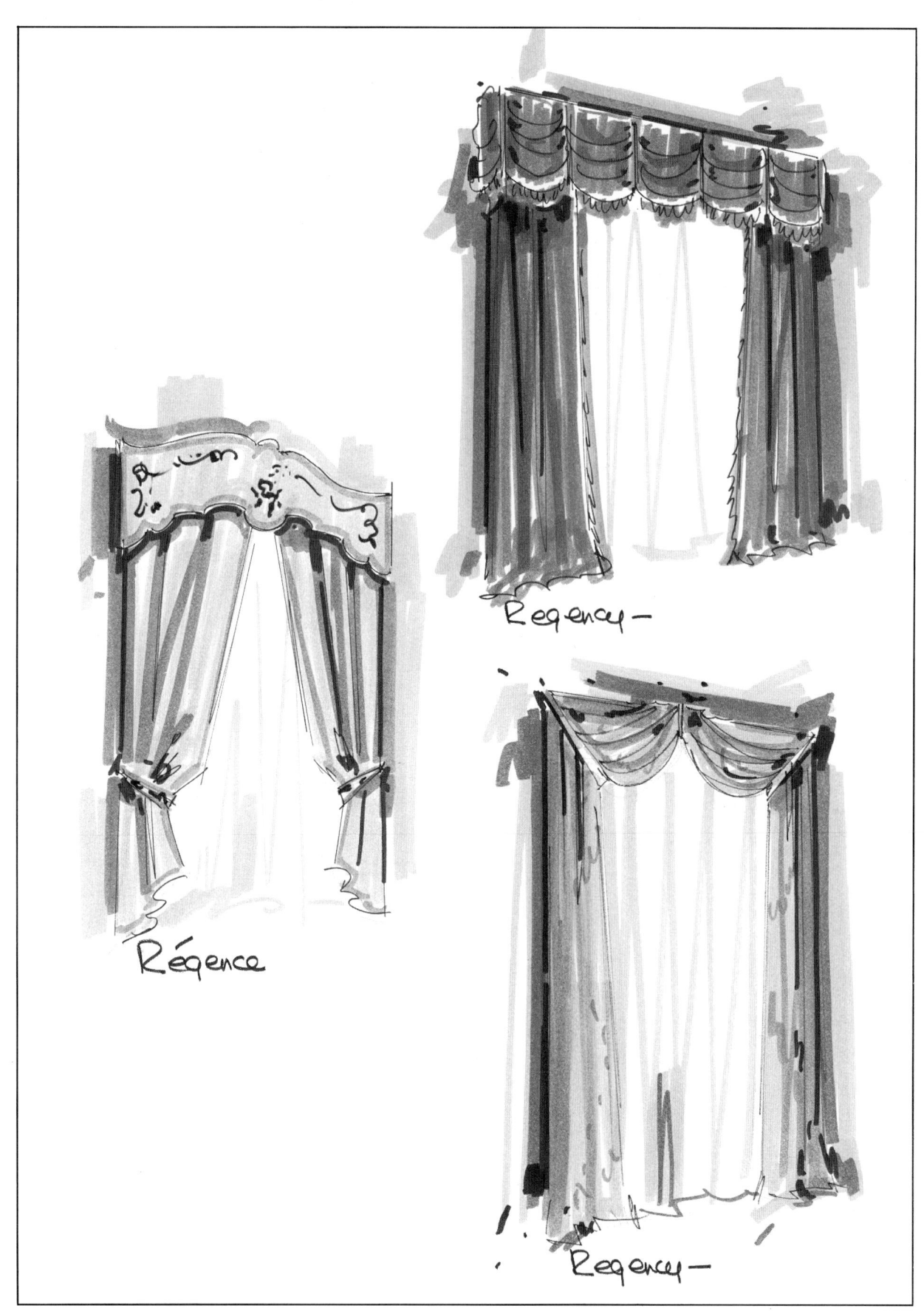

Regency

Regency

Louis XVI

Louis XVI

Louis XVI

Louis XVI

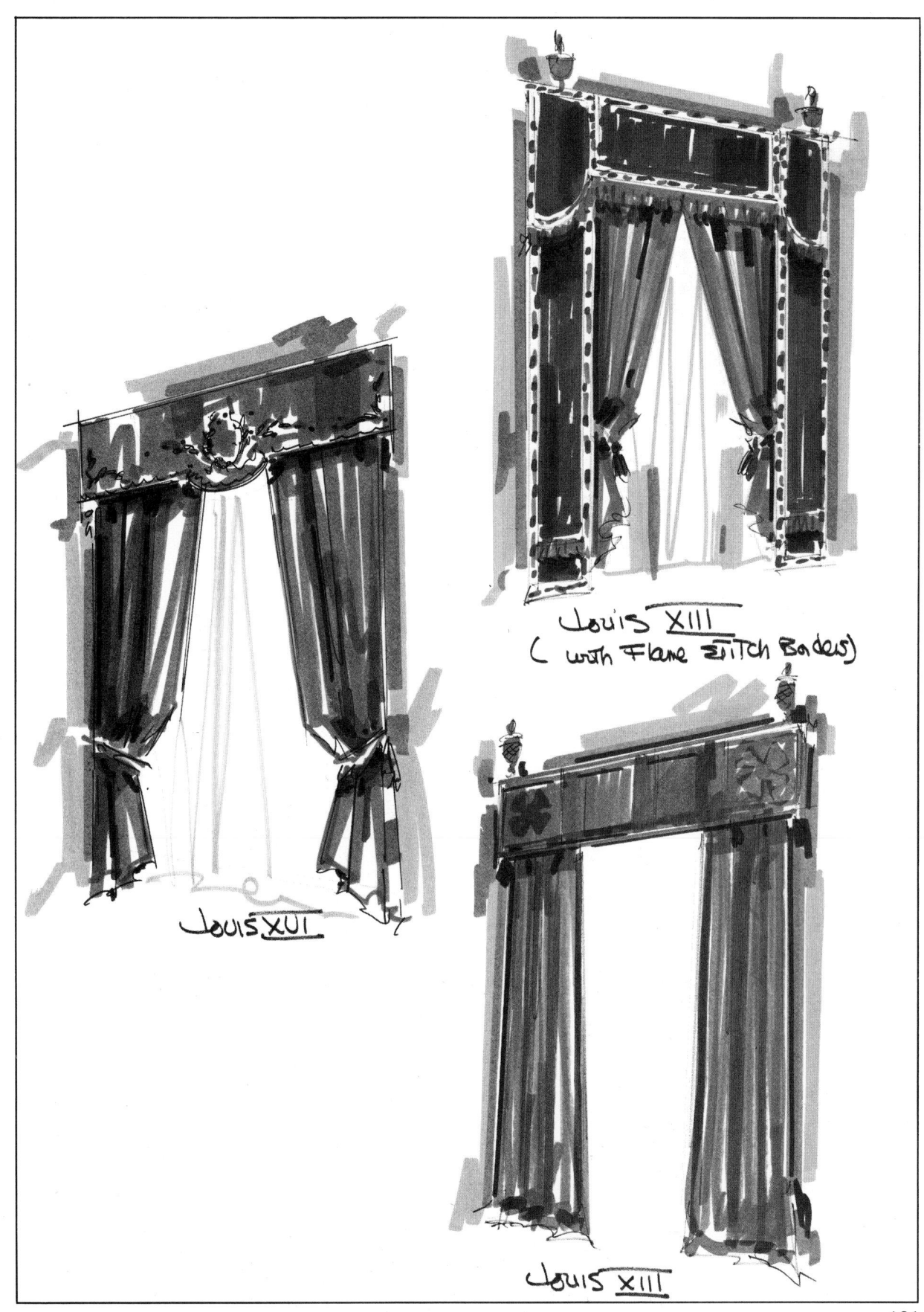

Louis XIII
(with Flame Stitch Borders)

Louis XIII

Empire

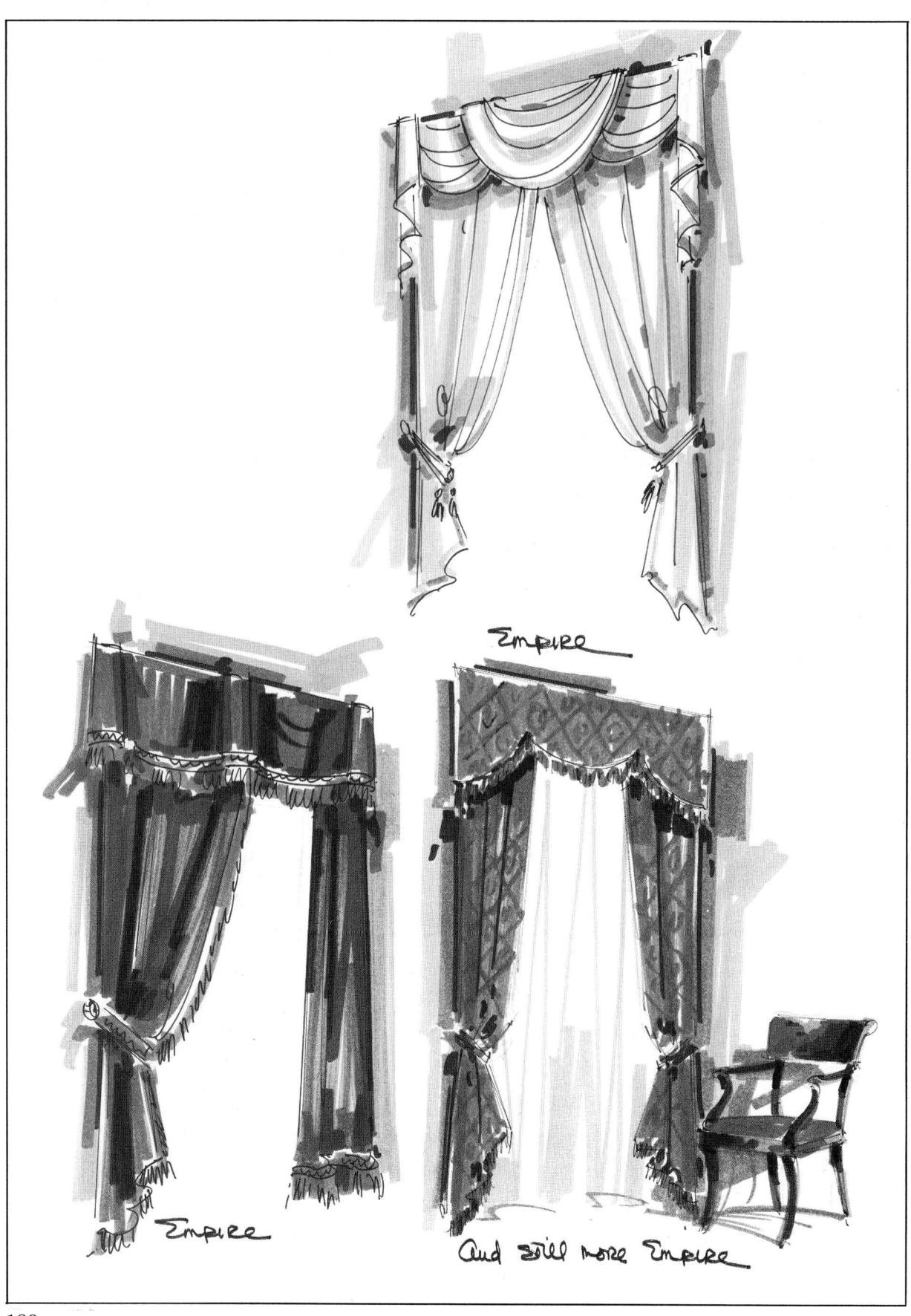

Empire

And still more Empire

MORE EMPIRE

LOUIS XIII

QUEEN ANNE
(Stencilled Damasks)

Chippendale – with the Oriental Influence

Chapter 7

How to Make Your Own Window Treatments for Every Room in the Home

How to Make Your Own Window Treatments

On the following pages, you will find some simple instructions on how to create your own custom window decorations. I hope you've read the rest of the book first, so that ideas are already stewing around in your head. Then you'll have more mix-and-match inspirations as you read through these directions and visualize custom combinations for every room in your home!

You can cover an air conditioner with a simple lattice frame, which I'll show you how to make as easily as 1-2-3. You can create your own stained-glass window with a pair of scissors, some masking tape, and colored acetate available at any art supply store, most department stores, and even some toy stores.

You'll find you can create a window wall of floor-to-ceiling panels, painted in bright colors or filled in with exquisite fabric or paper of your choice. Decorating ideas like these can create moods and tones for your rooms that range from a quiet country atmosphere to pure elegance.

One last word: The how-to's that follow are on making window *frames*. If your taste runs to valances, simply follow my instructions for making frames but omit the sides and foot of the frame—and, you will have a valance! To be really creative, and with no more effort on your part, that valance or frame can be cut by your lumberyard to your specifications in shapes—curves, geometrics, even see-through cutouts!

So get out your sketchbook and your tape measure, and get to work!

How to Make Pinch-Pleated Draperies

Pinch-pleated draperies are easy to sew at home. Just follow these steps:

1. Measure drapery rod and double that figure to determine what width the draperies should be.

2. Figure out the number of panels you'll need by dividing the width figure by the width of your fabric, minus two 2-inch seam allowances. Say, for example, your window is 99 inches wide. You'll need 198 inches of fabric. If the fabric you're using is 36 inches wide, divide 198 by 32. You'll need six 32-inch panels.

To find out how much material to buy, multiply the number of panels by the length measurement (height floor-to-ceiling for full-length draperies, plus 7 inches for hems and heading). Divide resulting figure by 36 to convert to yards.

3. Cut out fabric on a flat surface, cutting just one panel first and using that panel as a pattern for the others.

Cut lining material 3 1/2 inches shorter and 6 inches narrower than the drapery panel.

4. Hem draperies and lining separately. On draperies, make a 3-inch hem, double it over, and then hem again. Total depth should be 6 inches.

5. Place lining and drapery fabrics right sides together, raw top edges flush. Center lining so there's a 1 1/4-inch hem on either side, and stitch lining to drapery fabric. Turn right side out, and blindstitch drapery fabric hangover to lining.

6. Place commercial pleater tape and draperies right sides together. Stitch across top. Turn right side out, press, and stitch down along tape sides and bottom, under hook pockets.

7. Insert pleating hooks to make pleats. (The kind with a locking device is best for heavy fabrics, such as duck.)

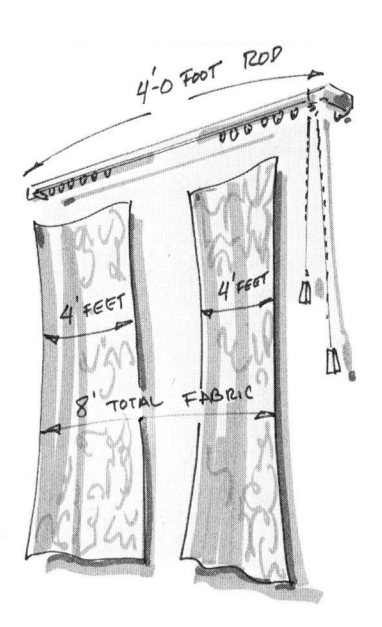

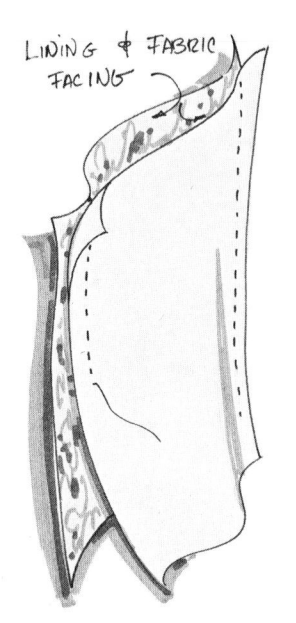

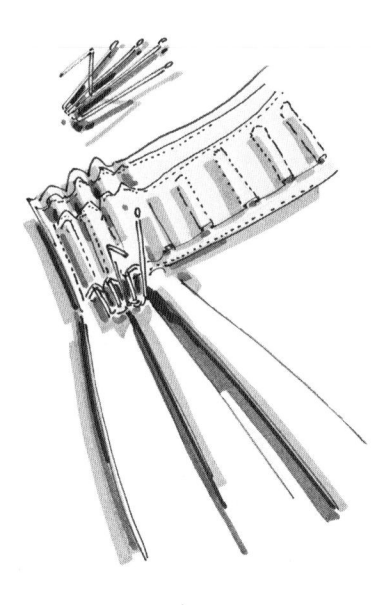

Step 2   Step 5   Step 7

How to Make a Paneled Screen

A paneled screen can be anything from an open-out scrim, set inside a window, to a floor-to-ceiling, fold-up showpiece. You can make two types of paneled screens: solid panels or frame panels.

For a solid panel:

1. Buy cut-to-measure plywood to the height and width of the space you want to screen.

2. Glue or staple fabric or paper to the front and edges of each panel. If you staple, staple only at edges, tucking corners as you would when wrapping a gift package. Spot gluing will help here. Trim excess fabric.

3. Seam a length of fabric, or cut a panel of paper, to fit the back of the panel. Staple or glue the fabric or paper to the panel. If you staple, attach staples as close to edges as possible.

4. Trim edges with wood stripping, braid, gimp, or any border decoration.

5. Attach hinges, using screws, not nails. Border decoration can be cut away at hinges for easy attachment. The hardware store will tell you precisely what hinges to buy. (Be sure to bring with you the exact width of your panel edge.)

Step 1   Step 2   Step 4

For a frame panel:

1. Buy stock lumber boards: 2 × 4's for a heavy floor-to-ceiling panel; 1 × 2's for a panel you will attach to a wall or window. Buy thin finishing strips the width of the boards; they will cover nails, hinges, and staples on the back of the frame.

2. Make your frame panels to fit width and height of the space you want to cover. First cut the boards to measure, then screw corners together with a straight or L-shaped metal plate. (The screws should come with the plate)

3. With staples or glue, attach fabric or paper to the back of the screen.

4. Finish with wood stripping of the same width—but not the same thickness—of the boards, using finishing nails.

5. You can paint the frame and the finishing strips before or after the fabric or paper has been stapled to the back of the frame. It's easier if you paint before.

6. With hinges, attach the one-frame screen to the inside of your window. If your screen is multipaneled, first hinge panels together, and then attach screen to the window or let it stand free. (See instructions for solid panel hinging, above)

Note: Sheet mirror can be very effective when used to cover a screen. You can buy precut sheet mirror and attach it with Velcro strips (see Glossary), or you can buy the adhesive-backed mirror and simply press in place.

How to Frame a Window in Wood (or in Fabric-Covered Wood)

1. Use 1 × 10 pine, cut to fit. Miter the corners, using a miter board, or allow corners to meet flush. (The latter is easier, although a little practice with a miter board will make you an expert in no time at all)

2. Using a straight or an L-shaped hinge, screw corners together at the back of the frame.

3. Using the same L-shaped hinges, attach 1 × 10 side panels to the front frame. Finish with a piece of 1 × 10 board across the top of your frame (it's not necessary to finish the bottom).

Note: *You can cover your frame in fabric if you wish. Simply staple the fabric to the frame as you're building it; hinges can be attached right through the fabric. See instructions on covering a paneled screen with fabric or paper.*

How to Make a Roman Shade

Roman-shade tape is available on the market with simple, easy-to-follow instructions on how to attach it.

Some extra advice:
1. *A tightly woven fabric is best for making Romans.*
2. *Cut the fabric some 4 inches wider than the actual window to allow for 2-inch side hems.*
3. *For horizontal tucking, 2 inches extra should be allowed for length.*

How to Make a Lattice

1. *First, read instructions on making a frame.*
2. *When your frame is made but not attached, nail slatting at measured intervals in a criss-cross pattern to the back of your frame.*
3. *Cut or saw off protruding slat endings, to trim.*
4. *Cover the back of the lattice with fabric, or, if you wish, leave it bare. Finishing is unnecessary for the back of the lattice, since it will remain stationary.*
5. *Attach lattice to wall (see Glossary) or window frame.*

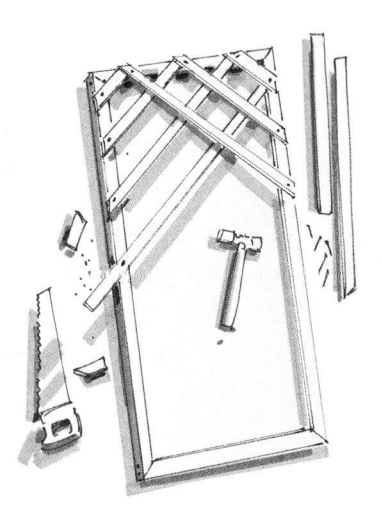

Step 2

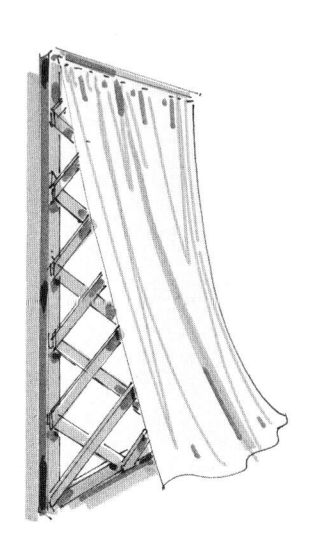

Step 4

Step 5

How to Make a Stained-Glass Window

1. Follow the instructions for making a paneled screen (only here, of course, you'll need only one panel, cut to fit inside your window).

2. Purchase lots of colored acetate at your local art supply store and some thin, black masking tape.

3. Cut out your stained-glass designs, and tape them to each other, around all edges, with masking tape. (You might want to lay out the acetates on a piece of paper cut to measure exactly the dimensions of the inside of your frame. Lay the acetates out and tape them; then transfer.)

4. Attach the taped acetates to the back of the frame.

5. Finish (at the back of the frame) with wood stripping and finishing nails.

6. With hinges, attach the frame to the inside of your window.

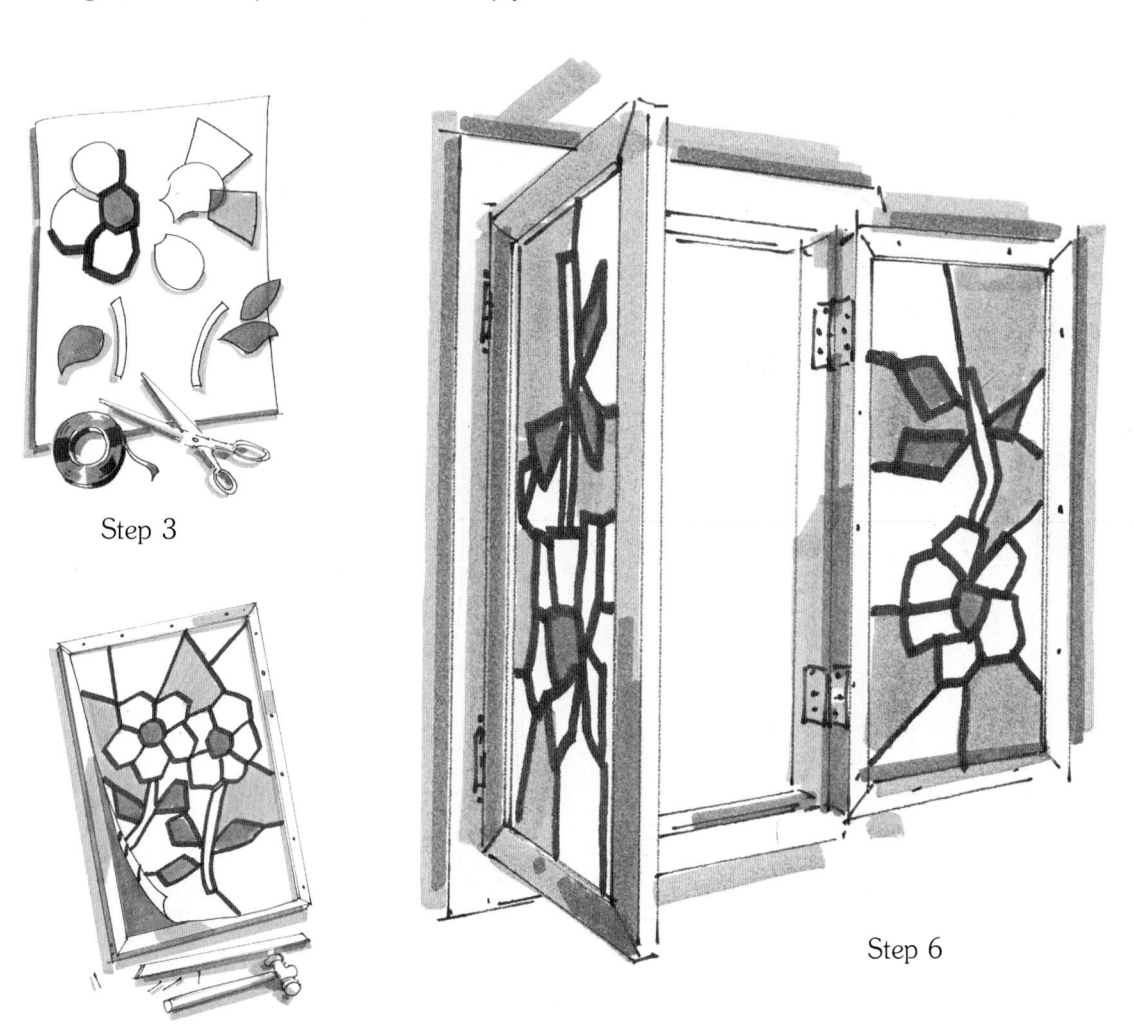

Step 3

Steps 4 and 5

Step 6

How to Stencil a Window Shade

With your own design:
1. Cut out the design you want to apply to the shade, using brown paper.
2. Apply it to your shade, using nonpermanent adhesive—masking tape that has been folded so that it will stick to both design and shade is a good nonpermanent adhesive.
3. Paint the whole shade any color you choose.
4. When the paint has dried, remove the brown paper; your designs will pop out in white.

With your wallpaper design:
1. Trace your wallpaper design on tracing paper with a stiff, heavy pencil.
2. Place the traced design on a sheet of heavy cardboard.
3. Press through the tracing paper as you redraw the design so that an impression is transferred to the cardboard.
4. With a matte knife (or razor), cut through the cardboard along the impressions.
5. Secure cardboard to the shade.
6. Using a stiff stencil brush and textile paint, work from edge to center until the stencil is filled in. Don't remove the stencil until the paint is dry. (If you wish to use the same stencil in several different places on your shade, first clean both stencil and brush. Again, don't remove the stencil until the paint is dry. Your patience will be rewarded.)
7. After 24 hours, apply an iron set on a low temperature to the shade, using a pressing cloth over the shade for protection. (If you want to stencil more than one color, a separate stencil must be prepared for each color. And remember, all you stencilers, that white, room-darkening shades offer the best painting surface.)

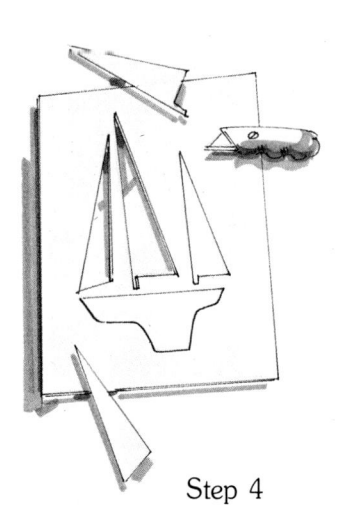

Step 3 Step 4 Step 6

How to Apply Fabric to Shades

Note: *Never, but never try to sew fabric to a window shade—it will ripple or bunch.*

For cutout fabric:
1. Cut out fabric designs.
2. Glue them to shade.
3. Allow glue to dry.
4. Paint edges of cutout fabric with colorless nail polish, to prevent raveling.

For solid fabric:
1. Trim fabric to the exact width and rolled-out depth of shade, leaving a 1/4-inch seam allowance.
2. Press seam allowances under, measuring carefully.
3. Carefully glue seams to back of fabric.
4. Allow to dry.
5. Working carefully and spreading glue evenly, attach entire piece of fabric to shade.
6. Allow to dry.

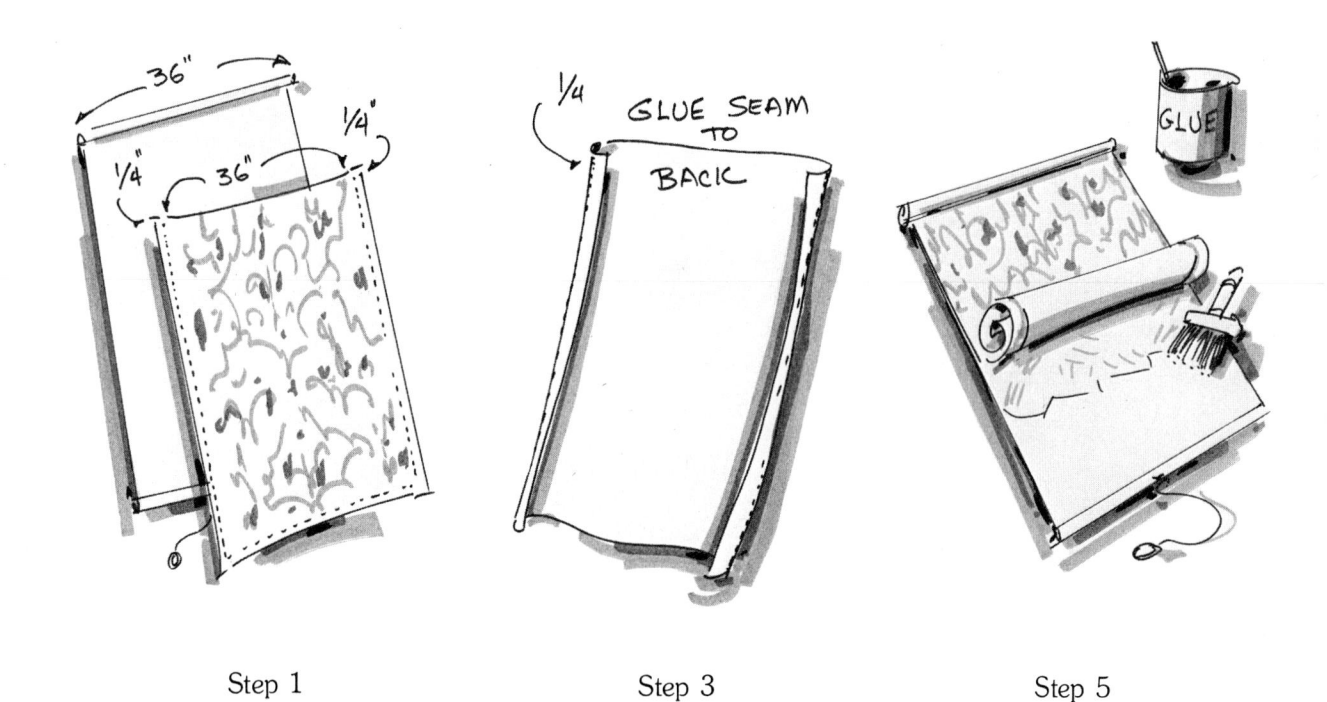

Step 1

Step 3

Step 5

A Glossary of Window Decorating Terms

Glossary

Anchor: A plastic, lead, or fiber sheath which, when inserted into a drilled hole, gives reinforced strength to screws or nails, either by holding them firm in a solid wall, or by expanding to provide tension in a hollow wall. See *hollow wall construction; solid wall construction; plug.*

Austrian shade: An elegant window treatment made of shirred fabric that gives the effect of vertical rows of swags and ends in a row of scallops. It is raised and lowered by a pulley cord.

Baton pull: A vertical rod that hangs at the head edge of traverse-hung curtains and that is used to open and close curtains instead of a cord, pulley, or push-button control.

Bell and swag design: A method of treating windows by looping and shirring fabric through and around a horizontal rod at the top of the window frame, allowing the fabric to cascade down the sides of the window.

Cornice: A plain or molded wood or metal valance, sometimes used to conceal indirect lighting. See *valance.*

Crown molding: Molding applied to the seam between interior walls and ceilings. See *molding.*

Crown valance: A valance mounted at the wall–ceiling seam rather than from the top of a window or cluster of windows. See *valance.*

Dado: The lower section of an interior wall that is paneled, molded, painted, or papered to contrast with the upper section of the wall.

Dead-hung drapery: A type of drapery hung so that panels can't be opened or closed.

Dormer window: A window set into a gabled niche or slanting wall, usually found in top-story rooms in traditional houses and, increasingly, throughout houses of modern design.

Double-hinged mirror screen: A movable screen to which sheet mirror is attached in lieu of fabric, wood, metal, or paper. See *sheet mirror.*

Dowel: A round hardwood peg that, inserted in drilled-to-fit holes, is used as a joiner.

Drop-down roller shades: Shades that are installed at the bottom of a window and that are pulled up on tracks to cover the window; they are most often used to create both light and privacy at the same time and for skylights.

Faux Bois: "False wood," in French. A method of painting surfaces so that they resemble wood surfaces or particular wood grains.

Frame: A finishing piece of metal, glass, wood, or fabric that finishes all four sides of a window treatment or three sides of a floor-to-ceiling window treatment. Frames are used as well to camouflage or incorporate other room elements, such as adjacent air conditioners, shelves, or radiators.

Half-round molding: A strip of wood with a semi circular outside edge used for ornamental trim. See *molding.*

Hardware: All decorative and utilitarian objects used to attach window treatments to walls and woodwork.

Head: See *heading.*

Heading: Any part of a window treatment that appears at the top of the window and/or the window treatment.

Hollow wall construction: Wall construction of plaster, composition board, plywood, sheet rock, or any thin, easily crumbled or cracked material. Most interior walls are hollow walls; to attach fixtures to these walls, a variety of hardware can be used. See *anchors; plugs; molly bolt; toggle bolt; molly jack nut.*

I-beam rod: A slim, flexible aluminum track rod, commercially available, that can be used to hang stationary, manual pull, or traverse draw curtains.

Jabot: The ornamental, cascading side pieces of a swag. See *swag.*

Long screw attachment: A method of attaching fixtures by which a long screw is inserted through the fixture (usually a wood fixture) into a wall anchor. This type of wall attachment is used primarily when fixtures have inordinate thicknesses and no special hardware attached.

Members: Pieces of wood or metal used to create frames, beams, or valances in a window treatment; also beams to which the finished wall is attached. See *uprights; studs.*

Milium: The brand name of a commercially available stiff fabric used for drapery lining.

Mitering: The process of cutting two pieces of wood, metal, or cloth at oblique angles so that, when joined, they form a right angle.

Molding: Ornamental strips of wood, metal, or *faux bois* that add interest or a period flavor to window frames and valances and that often adorn interior and exterior walls and ceilings. See *crown molding; half-round molding.*

Molly bolt: An anchor used for attachments to hollow walls. After a hole is drilled to size, the molly anchor is inserted with the molly bolt, or screw, in place. As the screw is turned, the ribs of the anchor expand. The screw is then removed, threaded through a hole in the fixture to be attached, and rescrewed into the anchor. See *molly jack nut; hollow wall construction.*

Molly jack nut: An anchor similar to the molly bolt, for use in fastening fixtures to thin, overlaid paneling, to plywood or composition board, or to hollow core woodwork; often used to fasten sheet mirror to a hollow frame. See *molly bolt.*

Mortising: A method of joining wood corners without hardware. Rectangular slots are cut in the edge of one piece of wood, and then corresponding rectangles are cut to project from the second piece and fit tightly into the slots. This method is also referred to as the "mortise and tenon procedure."

Mullions: Strips of wood that separate small panes of glass within a larger window frame.

Niche frame: Primarily used for bedrooms and bay windows, this frame both encompasses and integrates the window treatment and becomes a part of the room treatment. See *frame.*

Pelmet: An overtrim, cornice, or swag, made of wood or cloth, that covers drapery headings and undecorative hardware. See *swag; cornice; valance.*

Pinch pleat: A common finish for drapery headings, made either by hand or by application to the inside drapery head of a commercially available tape, into which metal pleat hooks are inserted.

Plug: A sheath wall anchor made of lead, fiber, or plastic, into which several different types of screws can be secured. Some plugs expand uniformly, others expand at the base. Both types can be used in either hollow wall or masonry construction. See *anchor; hollow wall construction.*

Plug and screw attachment: See *plug; anchor.*

Pull-down roller shades: Common, mass-produced shades hung from a round, semispring bar at the inside head of a window frame that can be raised and lowered by a pull. These shades can be appliquéd, stenciled, and laminated to create a variety of custom window treatments.

Roman window shades: See *drop-down roller shades.*

Ruching: The pleating, gathering, or fluting of fabric to form ornamental puckers.

Sash windows: Windows that open down from the top or up from the bottom and are secured in open positions by a tension cord, or sash, within the window frame. Newer sash windows have two panes, one in the top panel and one in the bottom. Older sash windows can be mullioned. See *mullions.*

Shaped valance: A valance made of wood or backed fabric that, instead of having a straight rectangular shape, is cut or carved in curved or geometric patterns. See *valance; cornice.*

Sheet mirror: Cut panels of mirrored glass, of standard or custom measurements, used for framing, screening, and valancing windows. See *Velcro.*

Sheet sliding window: A window mounted on head and foot tracks that slides open and closes horizontally, in the manner of a sliding glass door.

Shirring: The gathering of material in tight folds, either at the head or at both the head and foot, along two or more parallel lines of stitching through which a securing rod can be run.

Shoji panel: See *shoji screen.*

Shoji screen: A Japanese-style screen consisting, usually, of plain black lacquered frames hinged together and inset with decorated, translucent, or opaque paper sheets.

Soffit: The underside of a beam or frame, sometimes seen above a window; it can be made of concrete, wood, or metal.

Solid wall construction: Wall construction of brick, concrete, cinder block, or other solid materials; these walls are usually found in basements, garages, and throughout some older houses.

Split-wing toggle bolt: See *toggle bolt.*

Stationary overdrapes: See *dead-hung drapery.*

Steel angles: Flat pieces of steel joined at right angles and used for fastening wood pieces together so that they will be perpendicular to one another.

Stock lumber: Lumber cut to standard sizes and available in lumberyards at cheaper cost than custom-cut lumber.

Studs: Upright construction beams to which finished interior walls are fastened. See *uprights; members.*

Swag: A lavishly draped garland effect produced by looping fabric around a head curtain rod or ring attachments; can be used in place of a valance or extended, in place of both valance and side panels. See *valance; jabot; pelmet.*

Tap-in anchor: See *anchor; plug; hollow wall construction; solid wall construction.*

Toggle bolt: An anchor for hollow wall construction. To use it, a hole that is slightly larger than the bolt is drilled in the wall. The entire bolt, with fixture and screw in place, is then inserted into the hole and the screw is tightened. As the screw is tightened, the toggle wings spread out in the hollow wall and secure the fixture. Toggle bolts cannot be removed once they are installed; the wings are permanently affixed inside the wall. See *anchor; hollow wall construction.*

Traverse rod: A curtain rod that is backed by movable cord tracks. These allow the curtains to be drawn open and closed with pulleys or, occasionally, with automatic push-button controls.

Uprights: Vertical construction beams to which finished walls are attached. See *members; studs.*

Valance: A straight-across or U-shaped finishing piece that is made of fabric, wood, metal, sheet mirror, glass, or other ornamentation and that is hung above draperies to hide headings and to unify a window treatment. See *swag; jabot; pelmet; cornice.*

Velcro: The brand name for a sturdy fabric–plastic adhesive that can be glued to most surfaces. See *sheet mirror.*

Venetian blinds: Shades composed of horizontal metal or wood slats through which cord, ending in a pulley, is threaded. This enables the shades to be raised, lowered, and adjusted on inclines to admit varying degrees of light and air.

Vertical blinds: Venetian blinds made of vertical, as opposed to horizontal, metal or wood slats. See *venetian blinds.*

Index

Air conditioners, 27, 45, 78
Appliqués, 26
Arched valance, 106
Arched windows, 30, 106
Austrian shades, 74, 76, 98, 99

Bathroom windows, 83-90
    blinds for, 86
    children's, 88
    color combinations for, 83, 84, 86
    plants in, 85
    stained glass, 84
Bay windows, 25, 94
    curtain rod for, 97
    formal, 99
    lattice around, 95
    matching wallpaper for, 100
    overdraperies for, 96
    shades for, 96, 98, 99
    valance for, 25, 96, 98
Beads, 33
Bedroom windows, 43-62
    bed alcove and, 48, 59
    with blinds, 51, 60
    classic, 44
    with curtains, 52, 54, 56
    in Empire style, 61
    modern, 45
    with panels, 49
    with pelmet design, 51
    picture window, 48, 49, 57, 60
    with screens, 53
    with shades, 45, 48, 52
    with shelves, 50
    with stripes, 47, 58
    in teen-ager's room, 58
    with valance, 55, 56
Blackout shades, 44
Blinds, 12
    for bathroom, 86
    for bedroom, 51, 60
    for dining room, 64, 79
    for kitchen, 78
    for living room, 21, 28, 31, 33, 34
    matchstick, 31, 33, 34
    vertical, 12, 21, 28, 79
Bow valance, 55
Brocade, 19

Cafe curtains, 19, 37, 52, 63, 64, 101
Chains, 73, 107
Chintz, 55, 57
Columns, 24, 74

Cotton, 19
Crown valance, 56

Dining room windows, 63-82
    with Austrian shades, 74, 76
    blinds for, 64, 79
    with columns, 74
    curtains for, 67
    curved valance frame for, 71
    louvers for, 64
    screens for, 64
    with soffit and side panels, 75
    wallpaper borders for, 66
Doors, windows in, 76, 77
Dormer rooms, 104, 105
Dormer windows, 101, 104, 106
Draperies,
    (see specific rooms or types of drapery)
Draw draperies, 38

Early American windows, 19, 20
Empire style, 61
Empire valance, 71

Fabrics
    (see specific kinds of fabrics)
Faux bois, 22
Foyer, 21
Framing of windows, 129

Gadsky's Tavern (Virginia), 32
Gingham, 20
Glass door windows, 107, 108
Glosheen, 27

Imperial valance, 98
Indian prints, 20

Jabot valance, 99

Kitchen windows, 63-82
    air conditioners in, 78
    blinds for, 78
    curtains for, 63, 64, 68, 73, 78
    pelmet for, 70
    plants in, 73
    shades for, 69, 72, 80
    with shelves, 73
    shutters for, 78
    stained glass, 68

Lattice, 95, 130
Living room windows, 19-42
   with air conditioner, 27
   with appliqués, 26
   arched, 30
   bay window, 25
   with blinds, 21, 28, 31, 33, 34
   with built-in units, 27, 34
   classic, 24
   Early American, 19, 20
   fabrics for, 19-21
   with garden look, 36
   with glass beads, 33
   in log cabin, 40
   to patio, 35
   period, 19, 34,
   with pine planks, 23
   rustic, 19, 22
   with screens, 20, 35
   with shades, 20, 29, 32, 35, 36
   with shutters, 20
Log cabins, 40
Louis XIV windows, 19
Louvers, 44, 64, 101

Matchstick blinds, 31, 33, 34
Mirrors, 24, 35

Organdy curtains, 54, 68

Pelmet design, 51, 70
Period styles, 19, 34
Picture windows, 33, 48, 49, 57, 60
Pinch-pleated draperies, 30, 127
Plants, 73, 85
Priscilla curtains, 87

Roller shades, 33, 35, 36, 86
Roman shades, 29, 32, 80, 92, 96, 130

Screens, 16, 20, 35, 53, 64, 128, 129
Shades, 33
   Austrian, 74, 76, 98, 99
   for bay windows, 96, 98, 99
   for bedroom windows, 45, 48, 52
   blackout, 44
   fabric applied to, 133
   for kitchen windows, 69, 72, 80
   laminated, 20
   for living room windows, 20, 29, 32, 35, 36
   painting on, 31
   roller, 33, 35, 36, 86
   Roman, 29, 32, 80, 92, 96, 130
   stenciling on, 132
Shaped valance, 12, 104
Shelves, 50, 73
Shutters, 20, 78, 106
Silk, 34, 67
Skylights, 102, 103
Slanted windows, 92
Soffits, 75
Stained glass windows, 68, 84, 131
Stenciling on window shades, 132
Stucco walls, 19
Sunburst arch, 93
Swags, 19, 99

Teen-ager's room, 58
Tieback draperies, 12, 20

Valances
   arched, 106
   for bay windows, 25, 96, 98
   for bedroom windows, 55, 56
   bow, 55
   crown, 56
   for dormer windows, 104
   Empire, 71
   fabrics for, 20
   Imperial, 98
   jabot, 99
   pine plank, 23
   Roman shade, 32
   shaped, 12, 104
   sheet mirrors for, 16
   swag, 19
   walnut, 38
Velvet, 19
Vertical blinds, 12, 21, 28, 79
Victorian windows, 19

Wallpaper, 22, 66, 100
White duck drapery, 22
Window seats, 105